The Historic
Mars Hill Anderson Rosenwald School

"Our Story, This Place"

Notated History created by Friends of the Mars Hill Anderson Rosenwald School and the Mars Hill Anderson Rosenwald School History Committee

© 2022 Friends of the Mars Hill Anderson Rosenwald School

Pisgah Press was established in 2011 to publish and promote works of quality offering original ideas and insight into the human condition, the realm of knowledge, and the world around us.

Copyright © 2022 Pisgah Press
Printed in the United States of America

Published by Pisgah Press, LLC
PO Box 9663, Asheville, NC 28815
www.pisgahpress.com

Book & Cover Design
Simone Bouyer's Ad World Services
www.quickbrightsharp.com

Text compiled by the Mars Hill Anderson Rosenwald School History Committee:
Richard Dillingham, Dan Slagle, Sarah Weston Hart, and the late
Pauline Cheek, Charity Ray, and Dorothy Coone.
Individual stories and memories by alumni, friends, and descendants.

All rights reserved. No part of this publication may be reproduced, stored in a retrieval system, or transmitted, in any form or by any means, electronic, mechanical, photocopying, recording, or otherwise, without the prior written permission of Pisgah Press, except in the case of quotations in critical articles or reviews.

Library of Congress Cataloging-in-Publication Data
Mars Hill Anderson Rosenwald History Committee/
The Historic Mars Hill Anderson Rosenwald School: Our Story, This Place

Library of Congress Control Number: 2022945190

Includes illustrations

ISBN-13: 978-1942016731

First Edition
First Printing
August 2022

Our Story, This Place
NOTATED HISTORY

Prepared in support of the rehabilitation
of the Mars Hill Anderson Rosenwald School.

Acknowledgments

To the numerous hands that contributed to this project, thank you!

History Committee: Richard Dillingham, Dan Slagle, Sarah Hart,
Pauline Cheek (deceased), Dorothy Coone (deceased), and Charity Ray (deceased)

Fatimah´ Shabazz photo collection

Sarah Roland Weston Hart photo collection

Simone Bouyer, Webmaster

Manuel Briscoe (deceased)

Teresa Buckner

Edwin B. Cheek

Scott Donald

Sarah Hart

Ryan Phillips

Augusta Ray

Shirley Sewell (deceased)

A.D. Reed, Editor, Publisher

Les Reker

Oralene Simmons

David & Willa Wyatt

Madison County Board of Education

Mars Hill University

Cameron Huntley and *Mountain Xpress*

Helen Tarasov Reed Memorial Fund

Superintendent Will Hoffman

Members and supporters of the Friends Group

And the generous contributions of so many others!

Our Story, This Place

Contents

Preface vii
    Introduction viii
        Dan Slagle viii
    David and Willa Plemmons Wyatt ix
        Richard Dillingham ix
    Forward: Our Story, This Place x

Blacks & Whites in Madison County   **1**
    Master/Slave Relations in Madison County 2
    Blacks and Whites in the Greater Mars Hill Area 3
    The Story of Joe Anderson 4
    Race Relations in Madison County 6
    The Long Ridge "Colored" Community 7
    Mount Olive Baptist Church 8
        Mount Olive Missionary Baptist Church Congregation, 1960s 9
    Mars Hill Rosenwald School Stands as Living History of the Segregation Era 10
    Thelma Briscoe Harrison 12

Education and Rosenwald Schools   **15**
    Madison County Community Schools 16
    Public Education in Madison County after the Civil War 17
    African American Public Education in Madison County 18
        1905 Mars Hill Colored School Persons 19
    Julius Rosenwald 20
    Booker T. Washington 21
    The Vision of Dr. Booker T. Washington & Mr. Julius Rosenwald 22
        Overview of the Rosenwald Program 23
        The Rosenwald Schools and Black Education in North Carolina 24
    Securing Funds to Build a Rosenwald School 25
        Rosenwald Name 26
        Support from the Long Ridge Community 26
    Madison County Black Community Families: 1930 & 1940 Federal Census 27
    The New Long Ridge Rosenwald School Building 28
    The Long Ridge Rosenwald School, 1929–1959 29
        Mary Jane Katherine Haynes Wilson 29

Memories and Stories   **33**

    A Visit from John D. Rockefeller, Jr..34
    Arts and Crafts in the Long Ridge School...35
        Shirley (Barnette) Sewell 35
        Augusta (Briscoe) Ray 35
        Manuel Briscoe 35
    The Water Story on Long Ridge 36
        Black Folkways in Madison County: Doctors...................................36
    Black Home Remedies of the Briscoes...37
    Hands-on Learning Had Long Roots...38
        Manuel Briscoe 38
        Augusta Ray 39
    Viola Barnette, Crusader for Black Education 40
        Black Politics in Madison County..42
    Shirley Sewell 43
    Flora "Flo" Young Barnette 44
    Memories of Family, Community, and School...45
    A Teacher Remembers...48
    Charity Ray Remembers Student Life 49
    Reflecting on Changes 50

Integration   **55**

    Madison County, North Carolina Board of Education Minutes Related to the Mars Hill Colored School..........56
    Story of the School Building after Integration 58
    Lasting Memories..59
    Charity Ray Remembers the Long Ride to Education.................................60

Notable Biographies   **63**

    Long Ridge Community Achievers 64
        Kevin Barnette 64
        Dr. David Lloyd Briscoe 64
        Charity Ray 64
        Charlene Ray 65
        Sarah Roland Weston Hart 65
    Oralene Anderson Graves Simmons 66
        Oralene Graves Simmons Historic Connections 67
        Mars Hill University Honors Oralene Simmons................................69

The Billy Strayhorn Connection...70
    Lillian Young Strayhorn..70
    David Hajdu, Author and Jazz Musician..71
David L. Briscoe, the Boy Scout..72
Omar Lewis McClain: The Journey..74
Fatimah´ Shabazz: Walking My Walk, My Way..76
Rev. Dr. William E. Ray, Sr..78
Nationally Known Rosenwald School Alumni..78

At Rest   81

Legacy Families...82
    Joseph Anderson Family..82
    Viola King Barnette Family...83
    Remembering Homecoming..83
Local African American Resting Places..84
    Piney Grove Graveyard..84
    Mount Olive Baptist Church Cemetery..84
Other Known African American Burial Sites..86
    White Graveyards, Mars Hill Area..86
    American Veterans, Mars Hill VFW, Flag Memorial.......................................86
Black Graveyards, West Yancey County Area..87
    Roland Cemetery (African American)..87
    Remembering our Alumni..88
    Bowditch Cemetery, a.k.a. Billy Ray Cemetery...89
Manuel Briscoe Memorial Plaque..90
Viola King Barnette Funeral Service...92
Charity Ray Obituary..93

Preservation   95

Support Sought for Historic Schoolhouse..96
The Mars Hill Rosenwald School Rehabilitation Project..98
Friends Group Planning Committee Members and Contributors.................................100
What the Anderson Rosenwald School in Mars Hill Has Meant to Me............................101
Members of the Friends of the Mars Hill Anderson Rosenwald School............................102
    Scott Donald..102
Friends of the Mars Hill Anderson Rosenwald School..103
The Long Ridge Community Anderson Rosenwald School Strategic Plan 2013–2016................104
Greetings from Madison County Schools...107

Our Story, This Place Exhibit at the Rural Heritage Museum — 109
- Welcome! — 110
- The Mars Hill Anderson Rosenwald School Exhibit at the Rural Heritage Museum — 111
- A Pioneering School for Black Children in Madison County Finally Gets Its Due — 112
  - Cameron C. Huntley Obituary — 119

Local and National Recognition — 121
- Why Does This Place Matter? — 122
  - School Reformed — 122
- Resolution by the Madison County Board of Education — 124
- Mars Hill Rosenwald School National Registry — 126
- Rosenwald School's National Registry Now for All to See — 128
- Mars Hill Rosenwald School Reclaimed — 131
- The Story of This School Matters — 132
- Quilting Exhibit Honors the History of the Mars Hill Anderson Rosenwald School — 133

Appendix — 137
- Federal Census Data on the Joseph Anderson Family — 138
- African American History Time Line: The Long Ridge Colored Community — 140
- Water to the Long Ridge School — 144
- Time Line for Education in Madison County Area — 145
- Mixed Early Ethnic Heritage History of Mars Hill College[1] — 146
- African and Native American Ethnic Heritage at Mars Hill University — 148
- Peabody Education Fund in North Carolina — 152
- Schools for African Americans in Asheville, North Carolina — 153
  - Allen High School — 153
  - Stephens-Lee High School — 154
- School Books Recommended by State Board of Education for the Year 1886 — 155
- School Names Noted in Board of Education Minutes — 156
- School Committee Persons — 157
  - Known Mars Hill Colored School Committee Persons 1937–1964 — 158
  - Mars Hill Integration Colored School Committee — 158
- School Teachers — 159
  - Mars Hill Colored School Teachers 1901–1913 — 159
  - African American School Teachers of Madison County, North Carolina: 1924-1965 — 160
- Madison County School Expense Records — 162
- Notes on Integration — 165
  - Madison County Board of Education Meetings — 165-166

Preface

Note: Throughout this book, the terms "Colored" and "Negro" are used. The use of these terms is purely academic and made in reference to historical documents and other research. Today, the use of these terms is not encouraged or condoned and is deemed inappropriate.

Dan Slagle

Dan Slagle

Dan Slagle is a native of the Mars Hill area, having Madison County roots from the Pioneer Period.

He was educated in the Madison County Schools. When he was in the 7th grade at Mars Hill Elementary School in 1964, his class was integrated by his Black friend Michael Ervin, from the Long Ridge Anderson School. Years later, Michael's house, beside Mt. Olive Church, was used by Dan and the Friends Group for storing historic materials for rehabilitating the school where Michael, now deceased, was an alumnus.

Dan has served on the History Committee, leading the work projects for restoring the school building, including matching the original paint, hardware, and furnishings. In fact, he, Jennifer Cathey, Preservation Specialist at the NC Western Office of Archives and History, and several others are responsible for MHARS being listed on the National Register.

In retirement, Dan also finds time to serve as a leader in the Madison County Genealogical Society and the Colonel L. M. Allen Camp, SCV.

Further, he enjoys spending quality time with his wife Pam, their children and grandson, and fishing the mountain streams.

Introduction

The story of this manuscript is nearly as complicated and remarkable as the restoration of the Mars Hill Anderson Rosenwald School.

More people than can be named contributed to it, ranging from those interviewed more than 35 years ago by the late Pauline Binkley Cheek and her son Edwin B. Cheek, to those who have done yeoman research by delving into the archives of the Madison County Board of Education, the State Superintendent of Education office, newspapers, books, and other sources. From the early 1980s through 2018, Pauline Cheek took on numerous other tasks, such as researching, proofreading, editing, and interviewing, as well as transcribing twenty years' worth (1905-24) of Madison County School Board minutes from microfilm.

Especially diligent have been Richard Dillingham, a historian and researcher with unending appetite for detail and confirmable facts, and Dan Slagle, whose knowledge and understanding of original sources, paint layers, and other essentials (in construction and history) helped ensure accuracy in the school building's rehabilitation.

Such alumni as Fatimah´ Shabazz and Omar McClain, Sarah Hart, Charity Ray and her late sister Dorothy Ray Coone, Oralene Graves

Ryan Phillips and Dan Slagle

Simmons, and others have provided personal memories, documents, photographs, and other important information. And the entire committee has continued to hold the process in place as we have gathered and documented the material for this short history.

The committee itself has been led, convened, and glued together by the dedication and unending work of Willa Wyatt, who for more than 10 years has donated her time, energy, and leadership to bringing us together and keeping us on task.

The committee has also benefitted from invaluable contributions made by Simone Bouyer, whose title of graphic artist and/or layout artist does not encompass her full role in pulling these pages together, organizing and formatting them from scores of individual documents (Word files, PDFs, photographs with captions, lists of family names, etc.), and turning them into a book for our—and your—review.

We hope that there are few mistakes or omissions; but we equally hope that alumni, who are more intimately connected to the Mars Hill Anderson Rosenwald School than nearly anyone else, will catch any mistakes that exist and offer corrections.

~ A.D. Reed
Editor-in-chief, Pisgah Press
August 2022

Our Story, This Place

David and Willa Plemmons Wyatt

David & Willa Wyatt

David and Willa are both natives of Madison County. David was reared in the Petersburg Community and Willa in the Shelton Laurel Community. Both are graduates of Marshall High School. David and Willa both attended Mars Hill College.

David earned his BS and MA from Western Carolina College and his Ed. S from Western Carolina University. David was a teacher at Marshall High School, a principal in the Kings Mountain City Schools and Lincolnton City School. When David was hired to be a principal in Kings Mountain at the age of 23, he was the youngest principal in North Carolina.

In 1974, David and Willa moved back to Madison County where he continued his administration career as principal of Walnut Elementary, Hot Springs Elementary, and Madison High School, where he served for fifteen years. David became the Superintendent of Madison County Schools in 1990. Following his retirement in 1996, David served as an Educational Specialist in School Facilities for Padgett and Freeman Architects. He also served as the interim Superintendent for Haywood County School in 2002.

Willa earned her BS from Mars Hill College and her MA from Western Carolina University. During her tenure in education, she taught at Kings Mountain High School, was an elementary school librarian, a middle school math teacher, and a high school counselor in the Lincolnton City Schools. In Madison County, Willa was a counselor at Madison High School, Director of Student Support Services, and principal of Walnut Elementary and Madison Middle School. After Willa retired, she returned to work for a brief time supporting the beginning teachers in Madison County Schools and serving as an elementary school counselor at Laurel and Hot Springs.

David and Willa's children graduated from Madison High School, as did their granddaughter. Three of their grandsons graduated from North Buncombe High School, and one is a student at Mars Hill Elementary School.

Soon after David and Willa's marriage, they purchased a farm on South Main Street, which adjoins the Long Ridge Community in Mars Hill. Little did they know that part of their property had belonged to alumna Sarah Hart's dad, Arseamous Roland. In 1974, when they moved to live on the farm, their neighbors from the Long Ridge Community were the first to greet them and help them with their move. Charity Ray always invited them to the annual Mount Olive Church's 4th of July Fish Fry.

In 2006, David and Willa participated in Operation In-As-Much Mission project, sponsored by the Mars Hill Baptist Church. Stewart Coates led a team to clean up the ground of the Long Ridge School and his request was, "Need People Who Have and Know How to Use Chainsaws."

In 2009, Charity invited David and Willa to come to the first community meeting regarding the rehabilitation of the Anderson Rosenwald School. Following this meeting, The Friends of the Mars Hill Anderson School was formed and soon thereafter, Willa was elected chair of the Friends while David was designated leader of the Fund Raising and Grounds committees. Thus, began their thirteen-year leadership with the Mars Hill Anderson Rosenwald School rehabilitation.

The Wyatts were attending the 2012 National Rosenwald School Conference at Tuskegee University, when they heard that fewer than 15 percent of the 5,300 original Rosenwald schools remained. Although they were novices on historical rehabilitation, upon returning home, they were even more committed to seeing the Mars Hill Anderson Rosenwald School rehabilitated.

Richard Dillingham

My life has been blessed by the Long Ridge Community and its Christians.

Richard Dillingham

When I was attending Mars Hill College (MHC) in 1959-61, Big Frances, cook in the Mars Hill restaurant, fed me breakfast. I worked for Grace Gibbs, who gave me a room while I attended MHC. I would go to my room, and find my dirty clothes washed, starched, and ironed, hanging in my closet, or a hot cherry pie on my desk, with no name attached. I found out that Irene Ray McDowell, daughter of Avery Ray, was one of those women!

I have lived at the Forks of Ivy since 1938. On many mornings from my room, when attending MHC in 1959-61, I heard the Black men on the sidewalk of Mars Hill talk and laugh, saying "That's what they say down at the Fork."

Also, my understanding of Black local history has been enhanced by my college student researchers: Charlene Ray; Edwin B. Cheek; Stephen Chandler; Kevin Watkins; and members of our History Committee.

The Historic Mars Hill Anderson Rosenwald School

Forward: Our Story, This Place

Kevin Barnette

Kevin Barnette

Welcome to the Mars Hill Anderson Rosenwald School story, Our Story, This Place. I am Kevin Barnette, football coach at Mars Hill University, a native of Mars Hill, and member of the Madison County Board of Education.

My grandmother Viola King Barnette's letter to the Superintendent of NC Public Schools, gave access to high school for all rural children in North Carolina. Our Story is not just an African story; not just an American story; not just a Southern story; nor just a North Carolina or Madison County story, but all of these, and more! This is a Mars Hill educational story. So Welcome to Our Story, This Place.

Oralene Simmons

Oralene Simmons

I am Oralene Simmons, also a native of Mars Hill and alumna of the Mars Hill Anderson Rosenwald School, named for my great-great-grandfather Joseph Anderson. Joe Anderson was the enslaved man who went to jail as collateral in 1859 for Mars Hill University's debt on its first building. Also, I was the first African American admitted to Mars Hill College in 1961.

This history, Our Story, This Place, is also my story and the story of my family. My grandmother, Effie Anderson Coone, was a teacher in the Mars Hill Colored School in 1901. Welcome to Our Story, This Place.

Charity Ray

Charity Ray

Charity Ray of the Long Ridge Community in Mars Hill was an artist and church musician. Along with her sisters Christine and Dorothy, she attended the Mars Hill Anderson Rosenwald School. In fact, the teacher let her sit in when she was only five years old, where she drew her first art.

After retiring from Mars Hill University Education Department and Library, she continued her art with the Church Mice Art Group in Mars Hill.

Her mother, Augusta Ray, uncles, and grandfather Gilbert Briscoe served on the Mars Hill Colored School Committees. This history is truly Our Story, This Place.

Sarah Roland Hart

Sarah Roland Hart

I am Sarah Roland Weston Hart of Asheville. My family, the Arseamous Roland family, lived in the Long Ridge Community, and my son, Oscar Weston and family, still reside there. My father Arseamous "Seam" Roland was a school committee member of the Mars Hill Anderson Rosenwald School for eight years, 1957–1964, during the critical, but peaceful, integration period.

My siblings and I attended the Mars Hill Anderson Rosenwald School, and we are proud to call this home "Our Story, This Place"; therefore, welcome home alumni, descendants, and friends.

Our Story, This Place

Fatimah´ Shabazz

I am Fatimah´ Shabazz, daughter of Mary H. Wilson, a teacher at the Mars Hill Anderson Rosenwald School for fourteen years, 1939–1953. I attended this school.

In working with the Friends Group to save this historic school building, I have served as leader of our Alumni Group.

We hope that you enjoy this history, Our Story, This Place, and if possible, join the cause—also making this Your Story!

Omar McClain

Hello! I am Omar McClain from Marshall in Madison County. I attended the Mars Hill Anderson Rosenwald School and was bused from Marshall to the Rosenwald School, and later to Stephens-Lee High School in Asheville.

I too have worked with the Friends Group to save our school building, now listed on the National Register of Historic Places.

We invite you to visit and become part of Our Story, This Place.

Simone Bouyer

On behalf of the Historic Mars Hill Anderson Rosenwald School Rehabilitation Project's Friends Group, I, too, say Welcome! I am Simone Bouyer, a neighbor of the Long Ridge Community. I serve as Webmaster of our rehabilitation project.

The Mars Hill Anderson Rosenwald School is the only funded Rosenwald School building still standing in Western North Carolina.

Thank you for taking the time to travel through history with us to learn more about Our Story, This Place.

Lauren Rayburn

I am Lauren Rayburn, a member of the Friends Group. My family owns and operates the Rayburn Farm of Big Ivy.

I have served as the Grants Person for our rehabilitation project, securing the prestigious grant award for $50,000 from the African American Cultural Heritage Action Fund, one of only eleven Heritage Grants funded nationally.

This American gift makes each of us part of Our Story, This Place. Thank you, and welcome!

Fatimah´ Shabazz

Omar McClain

Simone Bouyer

Lauren Rayburn

Blacks & Whites in Madison County

The Historic Mars Hill Anderson Rosenwald School

Master/Slave Relations in Madison County[1]

> "Even though the slaves might have had a 'close relationship' with their masters, the lines of caste still prevailed…"

"An historian of Madison County has pointed out that the relationships between the slaves and their masters were generally a good one because the county was so sparsely settled and the slaves were like members of the family. They and their masters worked together side by side, in the field.

"However, working side by side in fields does not constitute a 'good relationship.' Even though the slaves might have had a 'close relationship' with their masters, the lines of caste still prevailed greatly, as the following story told by Everette Barnette clearly shows.

"'One day Everette's grandfather was looking at a book. White people did not allow Blacks to look at books; however, Everette's grandfather was just a boy. He was only playing around the house. He said that the hardest whooping he ever got, he got from the White woman. She personally beat him herself. He never looked at any books anymore until after the war was over and he was free.'"

~ *Charlene Delores Ray*

A Map of Madison County, North Carolina, prepared for Tennessee Valley Authority, Knoxville, Tennessee, 1934. The map shows the location of Ku Klux Mountain.
Map provided by Dr. David Gilbert, MHU History Department

The Piney Grove Black Church and graveyard were located on Walker Branch, adjacent to Ku Klux Mountain! The location was, most likely, the same site as the Ivy Colored School during the late 1800s, all being located on Paint Fork of Little Ivy.

Blacks and Whites in the Greater Mars Hill Area

Black and White families were living in the Mars Hill area when Madison County was formed in 1851. Ten White families and five domestic slave farm families were neighbors during the period of Mars Hill College's founding in 1856.[1]

Until 1851, Mars Hill was located in Yancey County, with the Yancey-Buncombe line crossing Little Mountain at Mars Hill. After the Civil War, the "Ku Klux War" devastated the social fabric of the local area, casting neighbor against neighbor, causing fear, arson, and even murder within the neighborhoods.[2]

Thomas Shepherd Deaver, one of the founders of Mars Hill College, organized the Union League in the college building to protect the returning Union soldiers and the newly freed Blacks. But many mountain communities remained Confederate strongholds and organized the KKK against the Union League.[3]

By the early 1900s, Black families living in the communities of Cane River, Bald Creek, Swiss, and Higgins in western Yancey County, began moving closer to Mars Hill[4] in search of educational opportunities, tenant farm family options, domestic work, or possibly employment at the college or in Asheville.

Gahagan Post 38, Union Army Veterans, MHC Campus.
Photo courtesy of Mars Hill University

KKK ballad, "Such Getting Up Stairs."

Bascom Lamar Lunsford, "Minstrel of the Appalachians," collected the KKK ballad "Such Getting Up Stairs" from Doc Sams of Laurel.[5]

Bascom's father, James Bassett Lunsford, was a Confederate soldier with "Men Who Wore the Gray for Texas," later becoming grandson-in-law of the "Old Shep Deaver" in the ballad. (Thomas Shepherd Deaver was a Founding Trustee at MHC, and a strong Union supporter).

Bascom's father served as a teacher at the school, 1876-1878, and again when son Bascom was born in 1882, (NC Historic Marker).

In 1859 Joe was taken by the Sheriff of Buncombe County as collateral for the college's $1,100 debt to the contractors for their erecting the first college building on campus.

J.W. Anderson contributed funds to build Mars Hill College. He and ten other Trustees also gave $100 each to rescue Joe.

The Story of Joe Anderson

The story of Joe comes to us from oral tradition, both White and Black. His history was first published by Ammons in 1907,[1] again in the 1930s by Carter,[2] and in McLeod's college history, *From These Stones*, in 1956/68.[3]

A video of the legend of Joe, *Bonded*, was produced in the 1980s and is historical fiction.[4]

Joseph and his family, Jane Ray, Andy, Neal, and Cordelia, were owned by J. W. Anderson, one of the founders, and secretary to the Board of Trustees, of Mars Hill College.[5] In 1859 Joe was taken by the Sheriff of Buncombe County as collateral for the college's $1,100 debt to the contractors for their erecting the first college building on campus. Joe was placed in jail at Asheville until the debt was paid.[6]

Eleven of the college trustees raised the money, paying the debt for Joe's return to Mars Hill.[7] Joe lived out his life on a small farm below the campus on Gabriel's Creek, being deceased by 1910.[8]

Oral tradition says that Joe may have helped make the bricks for the first building. Also, some say that Joe went to jail freely. This may mean that he went without a fight! The oral tradition claims that Joe was in Asheville's jail only a few days.[9]

Joe's master, J.W. Anderson, lost his chattel with the Civil War, after which he became a Baptist preacher.[10] Oral tradition says that Joe took care of master Anderson during his last days in Asheville.[11] After his death in 1910, Joe was buried in the Huff family graveyard. Joe's family gave permission for his remains to be moved to the Mars Hill College campus in 1932.[12]

In 1959, the Anderson name was given to the Rosenwald Anderson School in the Long Ridge Community.[13] His name was also given to the Civilian Conservation Corps (CCC) Camp in the 1930s on South Main Street in Mars Hill, Camp Joe.[14]

Mars Hill College 1909

Timeline Notes

The bricks for the first building at Mars Hill College would have been made 1854-1855 at Mars Hill. The first building was completed in the spring of 1856.[15] If Joe was born in 1838 (?) he would have been 18 years old in 1856. The $1,100 debt with the contractor was not settled until 1859.[16] Joe's going to jail must have forced settlement of the debt. Joe would have been age 21 when in jail at Asheville.

Joe's original headstone was embedded in Robinson Infirmary on the campus in 1935 by Mr. Tilson, Superintendent of Buildings and Grounds. This information was related to a writer by Mr. Tilson in the early 1980s and later confirmed by James Fish and Ellen Coomer in the 1990s. The headstone is a rectangular field stone, located to the right above the front door.[17]

Joe's first resting place on campus was below the drive on Men's Hill. It was moved in 1955 to the Oak Grove, above the drive near the cabin, now Heritage Cabin on the lower campus quad, for construction of a new street, Dormitory Drive.[18]

In 1961, Oralene Graves, great-great-granddaughter of Joseph Anderson, was admitted to Mars Hill College. She was the first African American to attend the school.[19]

Our Story, This Place

In 1977, Charlene Delores Ray, great-granddaughter of Doskey McDowell, the granddaughter of Joe, was awarded the first Appalachian Scholarship at Mars Hill College. She graduated from Mars Hill Senior College in 1981,[20] the first Anderson descendent to do so. Further, she graduated with honors.

In 1995, Namurah Simmons, daughter of Oralene Graves Simmons, graduated from Mars Hill College.[21]

In 1999, the Joseph Anderson and Jane Ray family was celebrated as one of the Founding Families of Mars Hill College.[22]

In 2006, Joe's Memorial was placed on the National Register of Historic Places.

In 2009, Shamia Terry, granddaughter of Oralene Graves Simmons, graduated from Mars Hill College.[23]

In 2010, during Founders Week, Dormitory Drive on the college campus was renamed Joe Anderson Drive, and a memorial to Jane Ray was placed at Joe's grave.[24]

In 2015 MHU students planted a Weeping Cherry tree in honor of Oralene Graves Simmons at Joe's Memorial.

In 2016 MHU established the Joseph Anderson Memorial Kiosk: From Slave to Founder.

MHU Delta Kappa Theta men's fraternity adopted the historic Anderson Memorial Site as a project for upkeep, beautification, and interpretation of Joe's story.

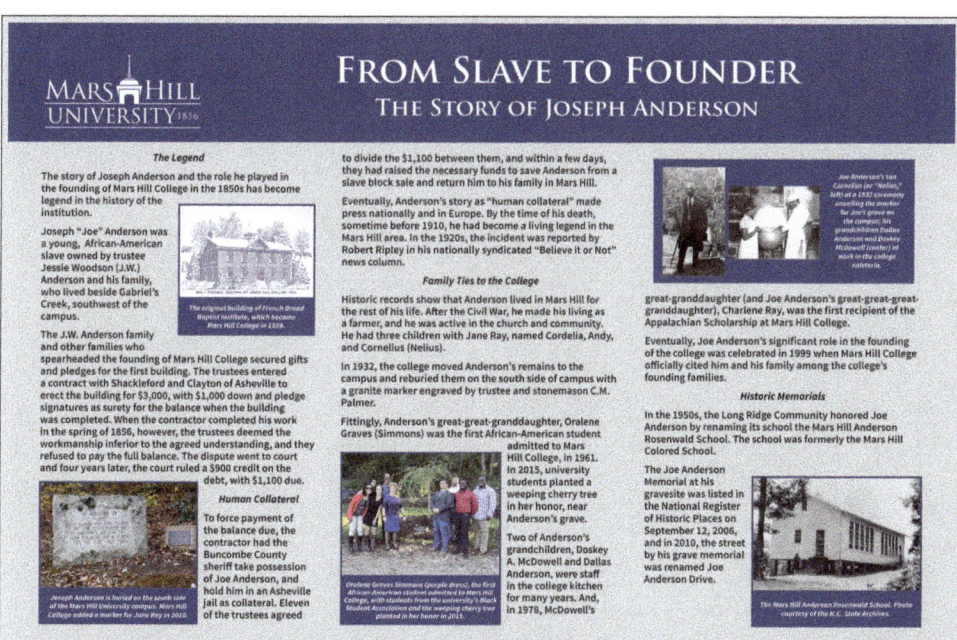

In 2016 MHU established the Joseph Anderson Memorial Kiosk: From Slave to Founder.

Effie Coone, granddaughter of Joseph Anderson.
Photo courtesy of John Campbell

Joe Anderson Memorial

Mrs. Gertrude G. Bruton, shown here in 2013 at age 93, attended the Long Ridge Colored School. Her daughter, Oralene Anderson Graves Simmons (R), attended the Rosenwald School. Both are descendants of Joe Anderson.

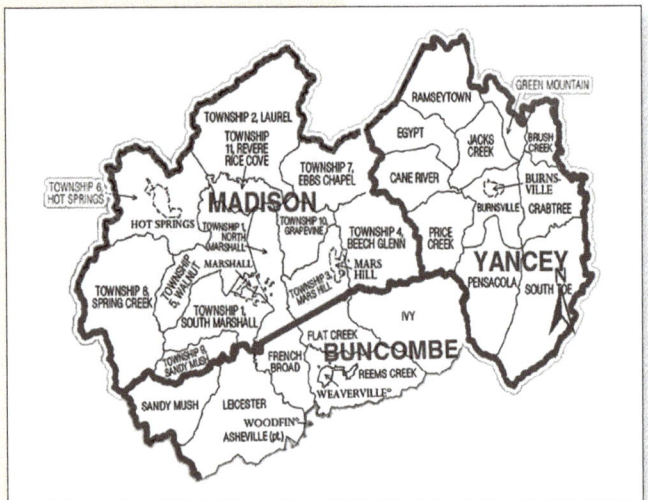

Race Relations in Madison County[1]

"Before the Civil Rights Act of 1964, Blacks could not sit down in any restaurant or café in either Marshall or Mars Hill. Blacks also had to sit at the back of the bus while riding to Asheville. The caste line was slow to break down in Mars Hill, and sometimes the line is still apparent, especially in employment and housing.

"The majority of Blacks interviewed in Madison County say that the relationships between Blacks and Whites have always been 'good.' … Perhaps one reason why the relationship between Blacks and Whites has been good is because the Black community has never been in competition with the White community. It has served as a self-sufficient unit, neither forcing itself upon the White community nor allowing the White community to be forced upon it."

~ *Charlene Delores Ray*

The Mars Hill Anderson Rosenwald School was named to the National Register of Historic Places in 2018. Ongoing renovation efforts aim to establish the site as an interpretive museum.

The Long Ridge "Colored" Community

The area called the Long Ridge takes its name from the ridge that runs from Little Mountain in Mars Hill to the Forks of Ivy. A horse-and-buggy trail along this ridge top developed during the pioneer period of the area. The ridge tops were passable even during winter.

Parts of this early road through the Long Ridge Community would become the main entrance road to Mars Hill from Asheville. This road has had various names over the years: Old Burnsville Road; NC 213/The Dixie Highway; Old Mars Hill Highway. Now, it has returned to the original name: Long Ridge Road, and South Main Street of Mars Hill.

Piney Grove Church on Walker Branch of Paint Fork in Madison County.
Photo courtesy of Augusta Ray

The Black community developed around two new buildings located at Long Ridge: the Mars Hill Colored School building erected in 1905, and the Mount Olive Baptist church built in 1917. School-age children were required to walk to the new school building if neighborhood transportation was not furnished. They traveled from Gabriel's Creek, Bull Creek, Banjo Branch, Bruce Road, Long Branch, or Forks of Ivy. Both White and Black children traveled by foot to their schools, walking two to three miles each day.

The original Black families in the Mars Hill area were the Andersons, Barnettes, Briscoes, and Rays. In 1929, the Madison County Board of Education hired John Ferguson for $40 per month to transport Black school children from the Marshall area to the Long Ridge School.[1] This was part of consolidation at the new Rosenwald School at Long Ridge in 1929.

After 1937, lots in the Long Ridge Community came onto the market, and other Black families from Yancey County—the Seam Roland family was one of the first—began moving to the community,[2] seeking educational opportunities, tenant farm family options, domestic employment, or the possibility of work at the college or in Asheville.

By 1940, the Long Ridge Community had fully developed. The Federal Census reveals that of the thirty Black families in Mars Hill, twenty were living in or around the Long Ridge Community.[3]

Mount Olive Baptist Church

The old Mt. Olive Church is shown in the background.
Photo courtesy of Augusta Ray

Mt. Olive Baptist Church in Mars Hill, NC

The Mount Olive Baptist Church in the Long Ridge community of Mars Hill originated from Piney Grove Church at Walker Branch on Paint Fork of Little Ivy in Madison County.[1]

The Piney Grove Church was organized April 6, 1906 by the Reverend Hamp Flack, with a membership of 100. Some of the organizing families were the Coone, Connelly, Ferguson, and Anderson families. The average distance for some to travel was around five miles.[2] It must have been at Piney Grove Church where the wedding ceremony took place for the marriage of Billy Strayhorn's parents in March 1910. His family recalled that it was in "wooded Mars Hill."[3]

As families moved closer to Mars Hill, they used monies from the sale of the Piney Grove Church property by Uncle John Ferguson for $120. Securing land near the school building, they erected their new church structure in the Long Ridge Community.

The church was organized as Mount Olive Baptist Church by the Reverend Sandy Ray of the Big Ivy Community, July 15, 1917. His support deacons were Harve Ray, Dolf Coone, Gilbert Briscoe, and John Ferguson, all bringing their memberships from the Piney Grove Church.[4]

Charity Ray's painting of Mount Olive Baptist Church was from a photograph of the 1917 Long Ridge church building.[5]

A young man from Sylva, NC, by the name of Joseph Smith, was ordained into the ministry and became pastor of Mount Olive Baptist Church in 1928. He met and married a local girl by the name of Cerilda Hampton and remained pastor there for 58 years until retirement in 1985.[6]

As families grew, a larger and more substantial church building was erected in 1952, bringing the 1917 cornerstone from the older building to the new structure.[7] Reverend Cleveland Martin, Sr., followed Rev. Smith as pastor. The Rev. William Hamilton has served as pastor and minister to the fellowship during the most recent period. Mount Olive Baptist Church is now a member in the French Broad Baptist Association of Churches.

Mount Olive Missionary Baptist Church Congregation, 1960s

Joseph Smith (identified as #3) became pastor of Mount Olive Baptist Church in 1928 and remained pastor there for 58 years until retirement in 1985.

Photo from the Augusta Briscoe Ray collection

1. Arseamous "Seam" Roland
2. Avery Ray
3. Rev. J.H. Smith
4. Manuel Briscoe
5. Edith Ervin
6. Gene Dobbs
7. David Briscoe
8. David Carson
9. Humphrey Briscoe
10. Frances Briscoe
11. Mrs. Humphrey Briscoe
12. Charlene Ray
13. Dennis Ervin
14. Donna Briscoe
15. Garry Briscoe
16. Denise Ervin
17. Lawrence Briscoe
18. Denise Carson
19. Tommy Briscoe
20. Lucile Hampton
21. Marjorie Briscoe
22. Margaret Barnard Felder
23. Ruby Briscoe
24. unknown
25. Edith Hampton
26. Lorreine Wilson
27. Debbie Wilson
28. David Lloyd Briscoe
29. Gudger Barnett
30. Augusta Ray
31. Frances W. Briscoe
32. Claire Roland
33. Sarah Roland
34. Mary Briscoe Davidson
35. Doskey McDowell
35a. Charity Ray
36. Viola Barnette
37. Lorraine Wilson
38. Debra Dobbs
39. Fannie Briscoe
40. Irene McDowell
41. Billy Briscoe
42. Emmitt Young
43. Bobby Briscoe

The Historic Mars Hill Anderson Rosenwald School

Mars Hill Rosenwald School Stands as Living History of the Segregation Era

by Paul Moon, The Asheville Citizen-Times, *October 4, 2019*

Effort to restore segregated Mars Hill schoolhouse keeps history alive.

After integration ended the school's nearly 60-year run educating children, the Mars Hill Anderson Rosenwald School building fell into disrepair. Neighbors tell how it was used to hang tobacco and as a place for kids to play basketball.

In late spring 1965, Lawrence Briscoe and his elementary school classmates walked out of their two-room schoolhouse at the end of Mount Olive Drive in Mars Hill as the last students to attend Madison County's last all-black school.

"It's great. I don't know if it looked that good when I went there," he said with a laugh while outside the one-story wooden building on a hot September Sunday. "It probably didn't. I'm serious."

Called the Long Ridge School by alums, in minutes from the Madison County Board of Education in the 1940s, it is named alternatively as the Mars Hill Colored School or the Mars Hill Negro School. A yearslong effort to save and renovate the 1920s structure has seen the school, still under control of the local school board, officially renamed the Mars Hill Anderson Rosenwald School. The moniker honors both Joe Anderson, a slave used as collateral during construction of what is now Mars Hill University, and Julius Rosenwald, a German-Jewish immigrant and Sears Roebuck executive who joined forces with education advocate Booker T. Washington to develop schools that by 1928 served roughly one-third of blacks in the rural South.

"It's history," Briscoe said of the importance of keeping his and other schools like it standing. "It's good to let others know what people had to go through in life to get where they wanted to go, and what they had to live through to get there. That's part of it right there—getting that education."

To get that education, Briscoe had to take the bus every day from his family's home near the Madison-Buncombe county line in the Forks of Ivy community. His bus driver at the time was his teenage cousin, Thelma Briscoe Harrison.

"I was just old enough to get a license," she said while sitting on the porch outside her family home located right next to the historic school building. "The superintendent (of Madison County Schools) asked my dad that summer, because everybody else, all the boys were gone that drove. They really didn't have anybody to drive. I said, 'Girls don't drive buses!'"

As the only viable option, however, she had no choice. Before attending classes at the segregated Stephens-Lee High School in Asheville, Harrison would pick up and drop off children at the Rosenwald School in Mars Hill and three other all-black schools in the area. Each day, she put 84 miles on the bus that she'd park outside her home every night.

"I'd wake up early in the morning for a child going to school, almost too early," she said with a smile.

When he arrived inside the simple white building with classic muntin windows, Briscoe remembers his teachers, Miss Brown and Miss Bass, stayed focused educating a room full of children ranging from the first to the sixth grade.

"They were serious about learning," he remembered of his teachers. "There were so many different grades in one place and you see how big that place is. You were crammed in there pretty good."

Reprinted with permission of the Asheville Citizen-Times

Our Story, This Place

Harrison also attended the Long Ridge School, just like her father Manuel Briscoe before her.

"It was really good," she said. "It was a family atmosphere, a real closeness with the teachers and a good learning experience."

Both Harrison and Briscoe said the reality of attending an all-Black school because of segregation was not something they dwelled on at the time.

"Especially growing up, we never did understand segregation and all the other stuff," Harrison said. "We were just people and everyone else was just human beings, too. It wasn't any different."

Harrison, who is retired and lives in the suburbs of Chicago, spoke with genuine fondness about her elementary school days.

Lawrence Briscoe was a fifth-grade student in the last class of Madison County's last segregated Black school.

"This is where we were, where we grew up," Harrison said. "Even during segregation, it didn't bother me. Here, we all got along just like brothers and sisters. We never had any issues. So, we just knew this is a school for us. We would still play with the White kids, it didn't matter. It didn't matter. We weren't brought up that way. It was just a lot of love."

While Briscoe echoed his elder cousin's sunny recollections, he also expressed a clear-eyed understanding about the mindset that dictated school choices for so many.

"We were just going to school," Briscoe said. "Even back then, we played with White kids. There was no problem. Even though we played with the kids in the neighborhood, that was good. They just didn't want us in the same school. It wasn't the kids, though, it was the grown folks. I'm just glad no one has to go through it now. That's my thing."

Briscoe lives in Asheville after more than 20 years of service in the U.S. Army. He came together with Harrison and other family and friends from across the country during the Mount Olive Church Homecoming weekend at the start of September.

"My dad, back when he was going school, he had to keep going to sixth grade because he couldn't go anywhere else for school until he was old enough to quit school. He couldn't go any further at the time," Briscoe said. "His generation couldn't go past this school. That's the reason it's important to tell people about this school. The Rosenwald School improved this community, the Black community, because when integration came, we were ready to move on."

For Harrison, even the school's name holds personal significance. Joe Anderson, the slave now recognized as a founder of Mars Hill University, was her grandmother's grandfather.

"It kindly holds the memories," she said. "My nieces and my children and my family, we try to teach them the history of what went on and they are so curious, and they are so hungry for that."

Dionetta Briscoe DeJesus is among that generation younger than Thelma and Lawrence. She came from Maryland to the homecoming this year for the first time. She said the experience of seeing the school and standing within its walls was invaluable, describing it as a tangible connection to the past for her and for so many Americans who are missing so much of their own personal family history.

"Even the millennials, and kids after, can see this and they can know exactly where we've come from," DeJesus said. "It's hard when you don't know where your history has come from, when you're brought over as a slave. You lose everything. Then to see where your ancestors have gone to school and where they've taught our children to become college kids. It's emotional."

Reprinted with permission of the Asheville Citizen-Times

Joe Anderson was the grandfather of Thelma Briscoe Harrison's grandmother.

Thelma Briscoe Harrison

Richard Dillingham interviewed Thelma Briscoe Harrison at the Manuel Briscoe Home Place on August 2, 2022.

An alumna of Mars Hill Anderson Rosenwald School, Thelma is a granddaughter of Doskey Anderson McDowell, who was herself a granddaughter of Joe Anderson.

Thelma recalled that her grandmother Doskey had told her that Joe Anderson had lived with them, and that Joe had given her a treasured gift [worth far more a century ago than today]: "a small cloth draw-string tobacco bag with two pennies in it."

Thelma shares her own favorite memory of her parents, Manuel and "Little" Frances Briscoe:

"Helping my father set tobacco plants between six and seven a.m. before driving the bus to school. My mother was like a mother hen, keeping us children under her wings. My father attended both the Long Ridge School and the new Rosenwald School building, while Mother attended the new school building."

Thelma herself attended Grades 1 through 6 at the Rosenwald School, from 1952 to 1957, and then attended the Allen school and Stephens-Lee High School in Asheville. Of the Rosenwald School, she says, "My favorite school memory was recess, because I loved to play baseball, first base, on the playground. Equally, I enjoyed the music by our teacher Mrs. Wilson, and the English class by my fifth-grade teacher Ms. Betty Sue Smith, who was from Kentucky."

She continues, "My favorite memory of the Mount Olive Baptist Church was singing with the Mount Olive Singers in the local churches, both Black and White." And as for the overall Long Ridge Community that she knew as a child, she says, it was "a close-knit, loving community, where all the children belonged to everybody!"

That's why she says about this place, "Keep this love of place alive, and pass it on!"

Thelma Briscoe Harrison has two daughters, Trina and Cassanya Harrison, who both live in the suburbs of Chicago.

Endnotes for Blacks & Whites in Madison County

Master/Slave Relations in Madison County, p. 2

1. "The History of Blacks in Madison County: 1860-1981," Mars Hill College Scholar's Research, 1981, pp. 3-4. MHU Archives, Local History, Box 1.

Blacks and Whites in the Greater Mars Hill Area, p. 3

1. John Angus McLeod, *From These Stones*, p. 20; 1860 Federal Census, Madison County, NC, Slave Schedule.
2. I.N. Carr, "Mars Hill College In The War Between The States," p. 4, NC State Archives, Box 76, Folder 76; copy in MHU Archives.
3. Lloyd Bailey, *Heritage of Toe River Valley*, Vol. I; Loyal Jones, *Minstrel of the Appalachians*, p. 4.
4. *Madison County Heritage Book*, Vol. I, p. 32.
5. KKK ballad, "Such Getting Up Stairs," Bascom Lamar Lunsford Collection, Scrapbook, Mars Hill University (MHU) Archives

The Story of Joe Anderson, p. 4

1. John Ammons, *Outlines of History of French Broad Baptist Association and Mars Hill College*, 1907, MHC Press, Reprint 2001.
2. Edward Jennings Carter, *A History of Mars Hill College*, p. 11, A Thesis for Master of Arts Degree, UNC Chapel Hill, 1940, MHU Archives Box 115, Folder 2.
3. McLeod, pp. 22-24.
4. Elizabeth Willard, *Bonded*, ten-minute video of Joe the Slave, Fletcher Foundation, 1986.
5. Ella J. Pierce, *MHC Founding Family Histories*, 1956, MHU Archives.
6. McLeod, Ammons, Carter; Elizabeth Webster Watson, *Bricks, A Play in Two Acts*, 1970 (Effie Coone was narrator in this play), MHU Archives.
7. Ibid.
8. 1910 Federal Census, Madison County, NC.
9. McLeod, p. 23.
10. French Broad Baptist Associational Minutes, 1862 (Not Listed as Ordained); 1873 (Listed as Ordained) MHU Archives, Box 112, Folders #2 & 3.
11. Anderson Family Oral Traditions, Black and White.
12. McLeod, p. 23.
13. Minutes, July 6, 1959.
14. Jolley, p. 46.
15. McLeod, p. 18.
16. Stephen Chandler, "The Story of Joe Anderson, the Slave at Mars Hill College," MHC History Paper, 1990, MHU Archives.

1880 NC Farm Census for Joseph Anderson, Tenant Farmer, Mars Hill[1]

- Value of all farm, $250
- 18 acres, Improved; Value $180
- Sorghum, 1/4 Acre
- Irish Potatoes, 1/8 Acre
- Implements, $6
- Corn, 400 Bushels
- Butter, 125 lbs.
- Eggs, 100 Dozen
- Potatoes, 12 Bushels
- Molasses, 22 Gallons
- Dry Beans, 2 Bushels
- Live Stock; Value $125
- Swine, 4
- Poultry: 6 barnyard, 6 other
- Horses, 1
- Milk cows, 2; Other, 2; Sold, 3
- Wood, 16 cords cut/used

> **In 2010, East Dormitory Drive on the campus of Mars Hill University was renamed Joe Anderson Drive in honor of Joseph Anderson.**

17. Bryson Tilson, Conversation with Richard Dillingham in the early 1980s, and Confirmations by James Fish and Ellen Coomer in the 1990s.
18. Jake Grigg, Contractor for Dormitory Drive in 1955, Conversation with Richard Dillingham in the 1980s.
19. MHC Laurel, 1968, MHU Archives.

The Story of Joe Anderson, p. 5

20. MHC Laurel, 1981, MHU Archives.
21. MHC Laurel, 1995, MHU Archives.
22. MHC Founders Week Program, October 1999, MHU Archives.
23. MHC Laurel, 2009, MHU Archives.
24. MHC Founders Week Program, October 2010, MHU Archives.

Race Relations in Madison County, p. 6

1. "The History of Blacks in Madison County: 1860-1981," Mars Hill College Scholar's Research, 1981. Mars Hill University Archives, Local History, Box 1, pp. 19-20

The Long Ridge "Colored" Community, p. 7

1. Madison County Board of Education Minutes, Sept. 1929.
2. Pauline Cheek Interview with Manuel Briscoe, 1984.
3. 1940 Federal Census, Madison County, NC.

Mount Olive Baptist Church, p. 8

1. Madison County Heritage Book, Vol. I, p. 32.
2. "Mount Olive Church Might Have Record Breaking History," Sentinel, March 17, 1999, p. 14; Herbert Barnette Collection.
3. David Hajou, Lush Life: Biography of Billy Strayhorn, p. 4.
4. Heritage Book, Vol. I, p. 32.
5. Charity Ray Collection.
6. Pauline Binkley Cheek Interview, Rev. Joseph Smith, May 14, 1986; Cheek, "Somebody's Prayers Must Have Been Answered," Sept. 4, 1986.
7. Cornerstone, 1917, New Building, Sentinel, March 17, 1999, p. 14.

1880 NC Farm Census for Joseph Anderson, Tenant Farmer, Mars Hill, p. 13

1. 1880 NC Farm Census, Madison County, NC, Mars Hill, Joseph Anderson.

Education and Rosenwald Schools

There were no schools for children of color until after the Civil War.

Madison County Community Schools

The first schools in the pioneer era of Madison County were "Old Field Schools," which were usually log structures erected by the community in an abandoned farm field. The log structure of the Heritage Cabin on the Mars Hill University campus was such a schoolhouse. It was referred to as a "Frog Level" school, built in the Grapevine Community in the 1850s.[1] Subscription Schools were held in these community buildings when public schools were closed down as the Civil War was fought during the 1860s. In Subscription Schools, each family paid the teacher in wheat, corn, bacon, or ham.

These community school structures predated church buildings in the mountain community. In fact, many churches in Madison County were organized in the local school building, as was the case with Mount Olive Baptist Church in Mars Hill. That the school building in the mountain community predates the community church buildings is an indication of the importance of education to the mountain family.[2]

Free public schools had begun in Yancey County in the 1840s with the North Carolina funding of the "Common Schools." The part of Yancey County that became Madison County in 1851 is included in that "Common School" educational history.[3]

It was claimed that North Carolina Common Schools were the best in the South,[4] and equal to those in New England. The North Carolina Literary Fund supported those free public schools for White children, but there were no schools for children of color until after the Civil War.

Our Story, This Place

Public Education in Madison County after the Civil War

Free public schools were reestablished in Madison County in the early 1870s, including "Colored" public schools. The State Superintendent reported in 1874 that there were twenty White schools and one Colored school in Madison County, with 860 White children and twenty-five Black children attending.[1]

By 1896, there were five Colored districts in Madison County: Marshall, Bull Creek (Mars Hill), Little Pine Creek, Middle Fork, and Hot Springs.[2] By 1901 there were three Colored schools in the Mars Hill area: Mars Hill, Grapevine, and Ivy.[3]

In June, 1905, Superintendent R. L. Moore reported "a school house built for Colored people at Mars Hill at a cost of $125 dollars, including an acre of ground[4]," located in what became the Long Ridge Colored Community, south of Mars Hill.

Known as James's Plantation School, this freedmen's school was created under the direction of Rev. Horace James on the Avon Hall plantation in Pitt County, NC in 1866.
Photo by John D. Heywood, courtesy of the North Carolina Collection, University of North Carolina at Chapel Hill.

1874 US Civil Rights Bill[5]

Passed by the US Senate, May 23, 1874

The United States Senate passed the Civil Rights Bill of 1874 on May 23, 1874. It read in part:

"All citizens and persons within the jurisdiction of the United States shall be entitled to full and equal enjoyment of the advantages of the common schools and other institutions of learning and benevolence without distinction of race, color or previous condition of servitude."

In response, North Carolina Superintendent of Public Instruction Alexander McIver replied, "I replied to North Carolina Senator Merrimon: 'No legislation in favor of mixed schools has ever been attempted in this State. Public sentiment on this subject is all one way: Opposition…"

> In June 1905, Superintendent R. L. Moore reported "a school house built for "Colored" people at Mars Hill at a cost of $125 dollars, including an acre of ground," located in what became the Long Ridge Colored Community, south of Mars Hill. [1]

African American Public Education in Madison County

By 1901, Madison County operated Colored schools at Hot Springs, Little Pine, Marshall, and in the Mars Hill area. The Mars Hills schools were fully integrated by 1965.[22]

Before 1905 there were three Colored schools in the greater Mars Hill area: in the Grapevine, Mars Hill, and Ivy neighborhoods.[3] The Mars Hill Colored School moved to a new building in the fall of 1905. The property, one acre, on which the new school house was erected, was secured from Mr. Scudder Willis in April of that year.[4] R.L. Moore, Superintendent, reported in June, "a new school house built for Colored people at Mars Hill at a cost of $125 dollars, including one acre of ground".[5] In 1908, J.R. Rogers was paid $10.50 for the road to the school, what would become Mt. Olive Drive.[6]

This new Colored school location was on a long ridge knoll, above the Ivy River Basin, overlooking the Forks of Ivy community, facing the Blue Ridge Mountains to the southeast. The Forks of Ivy was a crossroad settlement where pioneer homestead settlers and Native Americans left past and even ancient history evidence through oral traditions and artifacts.[7]

The Long Ridge name came from the ridge that runs south from Little Mountain at Mars Hill to the Forks of Ivy, along a horse and buggy road that developed between the two settlements. This road, over two miles long, ran through what became the Long Ridge Colored Community. This community grew around two new buildings; the school, built in 1905,[8] and the church, built in 1917.[9] The Mount Olive Baptist Church was built not distant from the school, close to where the church building is located today.

Mount Olive Baptist Church evolved from an older African American church, known as Piney Grove Church, located on Walker Branch in Paint Fork of Little Ivy.[10] It was in the Piney Grove Church that the wedding ceremony took place for the parents of Billy Strayhorn in March of 1910. This church was established in 1906, and the Strayhorn family remembers that the church wedding took place in "wooded Mars Hill."[11]

According to oral interviews with Augusta Ray and Shirley Sewell, they attended school in the older Long Ridge School building, as did Manuel Briscoe who also attended the new Rosenwald School building, but all three referred to the school as the Long Ridge School.[12] That local name continued to be used even after the new Rosenwald building replaced the older structure in 1928–29; however, the School Board still referred to the school as Mars Hill Colored, until 1959, when they voted to give the school a more appropriate name, Anderson Elementary School.[13]

The new name was to honor Joseph Anderson, the Mars Hill slave who went to prison for Mars Hill College indebtedness in 1859. The name may have been suggested by the Mars Hill Colored School Committee, according to members of the History Committee. Two members of that school committee were Manuel Briscoe, great-grandson-in-law of Joseph Anderson, and Augusta Briscoe Ray, sister to Manuel and mother of Charity Ray and Dorothy Coone.

Two Long Ridge School student interviewees, Augusta Briscoe Ray and Shirley Barnette Sewell, also told of a 1920s visit by John D. Rockefeller, Jr. and friends to the school. His gift added a new room for art to the building, the Rockefeller Room.[14]

By 1920, the Federal Census for Madison County lists 51 Colored children in the Mars Hill district, with 126 in the whole county, ages 6 through 21.[15] By the 1920s, it appears that the three Colored schools in the Mars Hill area were consolidated at Long Ridge.

1905 Mars Hill Colored School Persons[16]

Committeemen
J. H. Ferguson
Alfred Barnett
Neal Anderson, son of Joe

Teacher
Sam W. Anderson

Neal Anderson

Children in the Long Ridge community.

Julius Rosenwald

Julius Rosenwald, 1862-1932

"Throughout his life, Julius Rosenwald, with his distinctively Jewish name, took pride in his Jewishness, speaking openly about how his heritage had shaped him. When he declared that he hoped to alleviate in particular the situation of Black Americans, he argued that his attention to the people most oppressed in America stemmed in part from his Jewish outlook."[1]

Julius Rosenwald was the son of German-Jewish immigrants. He rose to become one of the wealthiest men in America by building Sears Roebuck into the nation's leading mail order house. But his most lasting legacy was as a humanitarian, whose commitment to social justice led to historic change for Black Americans in the South in the years following the Civil War. Influenced by the social gospel espoused by Rabbi Emil Hirsch of Chicago Sinai Congregation, Rosenwald used his great wealth and talent for leadership to try to fix what he viewed as wrong with the world. All told, throughout his life he gave away over $630 million to charity.[2]

"...Perhaps in no way was Julius Rosenwald more ahead of his time than in matters of race. After meeting Booker T. Washington, Rosenwald became increasingly convinced that Blacks and Whites were equal and should be treated as such. His most enduring legacy was the establishment of quality schools for African Americans. More than 5,300 were built in fifteen Southern states, and they lasted until the Civil Rights era.

A recent study by the Federal Reserve Bank in Chicago indicates that the schools had a significant impact on raising the educational level of the students who attended them. The schools helped create a new Black middle class in the South. Rosenwald hoped that if Blacks and Whites within the same community worked together to raise funds for and build a school for Blacks it would break down racial barriers. This did not happen until the Civil Rights movement advanced in the 1960s, and even then it took many years to erode the prejudices of centuries. But the schools were an important step on this road to equality."[3]

Julius Rosenwald with students at one of the Rosenwald schools.
Photo courtesy of Fisk University

Julius Rosenwald's grandson and biographer, Dr. Peter Ascoli, observed the following: "...His "Rosenwald Schools" were something really unique. Even the General Education Board, a Rockefeller Foundation offshoot (which was supposed to fund education for Whites and Blacks in the first decade of its existence from 1902 to 1912), funded almost exclusively White things because they were afraid of riling southern sensibilities. J.R. [Julius Rosenwald] didn't give a hoot about southern sensibilities. He thought that this was a great idea, schools for Blacks in rural areas, and he was determined to go ahead and it didn't matter what the results were going to be. And I think that kind of bravery and doggedness, if you will, was entirely admirable..."[4]

Booker T. Washington

Booker Taliaferro Washington was the most famous Black man in America between 1895 and 1915. He was also considered the most influential Black educator of the late 19th and early 20th centuries insofar as he controlled the flow of funds to Black schools and colleges. Born into slavery on a small farm in Virginia, he became determined to educate himself after emancipation. He was later accepted at Hampton Institute, where he became a star pupil under the tutelage of General Samuel Chapman Armstrong, the headmaster of Hampton.[1]

In 1881, Washington founded Tuskegee Normal and Industrial Institute in Alabama. He won the trust of White Southerners and Northern philanthropists to make Tuskegee into a model school of industrial education. He reassured Whites that nothing in his educational program challenged White supremacy or offered economic competition with Whites. He accepted racial subordination as a necessary evil, at least until such time as Blacks could prove themselves worthy of full civil and political rights.

As far as Blacks were concerned, Washington insisted that industrial education would enable them to lift themselves up ... and escape the trap of sharecropping and debt. Historian Robert J. Norrell believes that both the professional and popular wisdoms on Washington are seriously mistaken. Norrell sees a sophisticated mind, a complex approach to social problems, and admirable goals for the people Washington sought to lead, all in a world that set profound limits on what he could expect to achieve. Rather than take the potentially suicidal path of resistance or simply concede the fight, Washington offered hope and optimism, together with an effort to rise above history itself.[2]

Washington consolidated his influence by his widely read autobiography *Up From Slavery* (1901), the founding of the National Negro Business League in 1900, his celebrated dinner at the White House in 1901, and control of patronage politics as chief Black advisor to Presidents Theodore Roosevelt and William Howard Taft.[3] Gilded Age industrialists, like Rockefeller, Carnegie, and Rosenwald, who controlled the financing of many Black schools in the South, depended upon his advice as to which schools should receive funds. In 1903, Washington's policies received a challenge from within the Black community.

W.E.B. Du Bois, then a scholar at Atlanta University, attacked Washington's philosophy in the book *The Souls Of Black Folk*. "The legendary battle of ideas between Booker T. Washington and W.E.B. Du Bois at the dawn of the 20th century was also a battle over masks: should we seem humble and modest or prideful and outraged?" ...And yet both men had good ideas for Black uplift. Washington's emphasis on self-help was not fundamentally incompatible with Du Bois's emphasis on protest, and both were necessary.[4]

Most middle-class and working-class Blacks continued to hold Washington in great esteem. Even though he was known for a level of appeasement with White America, it was discovered, after his death, that Washington gave financial backing in many court cases challenging segregation.[5]

Booker T. Washington, 1856-1915

The principal of Hampton Institute recommended Washington to a group of Alabama legislators as a viable candidate for director of an African American school they wanted to establish. In 1881, Washington became president of that school, known as Tuskegee Institute.

In the 1900s, Dr. Booker T. Washington, world-renowned educator and founder of the Tuskegee Institute, knew that early education was needed for children of color.

The Vision of Dr. Booker T. Washington & Mr. Julius Rosenwald

Due to Booker T.'s personal sojourn, determination, and passion for education, a vision was born and a destiny was put into play. Dr. Washington and Mr. Julius Rosenwald, president of Sears and Roebuck, would meet, connect and take a stand for children of color.

Mr. Rosenwald already had an interest in supporting a wide range of charitable causes for Negro people. However, after reading Dr. Washington's book *Up From Slavery*, Mr. Rosenwald's chief concern became "Education for Negro children in the South." Rosenwald was motivated to work with Washington based on his belief in the value of education, combined with hard work and self-reliance, as the foundation for personal success.

Washington shared Rosenwald's vision about the transformative power of education. Together they created the Rosenwald School Fund, which had its beginnings on the campus of Tuskegee Institute.

Dr. Washington and Mr. Rosenwald met in person in 1910-1911, and soon Mr. Rosenwald became a trustee of Tuskegee Institute. Dr. Washington informed and persuaded Mr. Rosenwald that help was needed for children of color, not just in higher education, but at the elementary school level.

On the occasion of Mr. Rosenwald's fiftieth birthday, he presented Dr. Washington with $25,000 to aid Black colleges and preparatory academies. Dr. Washington asked that a small amount be used as grants to build elementary schools in rural areas near Tuskegee. Mr. Rosenwald accepted with the stipulation that each community had to raise funds to match the gift of the grant.

The first Rosenwald school was built in Alabama and dedicated in 1913. In 1915, at the age of 59, Dr. Booker T. Washington made his passage from this life. By this time, some 80 schools in three states had matched the gift of the grant. In 1917, in order for Dr. Washington's vision to continue, Mr. Rosenwald established the Julius Rosenwald Fund.[1]

Julius Rosenwald (left) and Booker T. Washington at the Tuskegee Institute in Alabama in 1915.
Photo courtesy of University of Chicago Library/Ciesla Foundation

Overview of the Rosenwald Program

The Rosenwald rural school building program was a major effort to improve the quality of public education for African Americans in the South during the early twentieth century.

In 1912, Julius Rosenwald gave Booker T. Washington permission to use funds he had donated to Tuskegee Institute for the construction of six small schools. Pleased with the results, Rosenwald then agreed to fund a larger program for schoolhouse construction.

By 1920, the burgeoning construction program to build the schools was more than Tuskegee could handle. Mr. Rosenwald then created the Rosenwald Southern Office, located in Nashville, TN. Mr. Samuel Leonard Smith was hired to run the Nashville office. Mr. Smith had decades of experience administering Tennessee's rural Negro school programs and possessed a keen interest in country school house designs.

By 1928, one in every five rural schools for Black students in the South was a Rosenwald school. At the program's conclusion in 1932, it had produced 4,977 new schools, 217 teachers' homes, 163 shop buildings, and served 663,615 students in 15 states.

Approximately 800+ schools were built in North Carolina. Each of these small communities was able to match funds from the Rosenwald grant to have a school constructed in their community. The vision of Dr. Washington and the well-placed investment of Mr. Rosenwald has given us a mighty legacy, one that lives on and continues to this day.[1]

Julius Rosenwald and Berry O'Kelly visit a NC Rosenwald School.
Photo courtesy of the University of Virginia Library

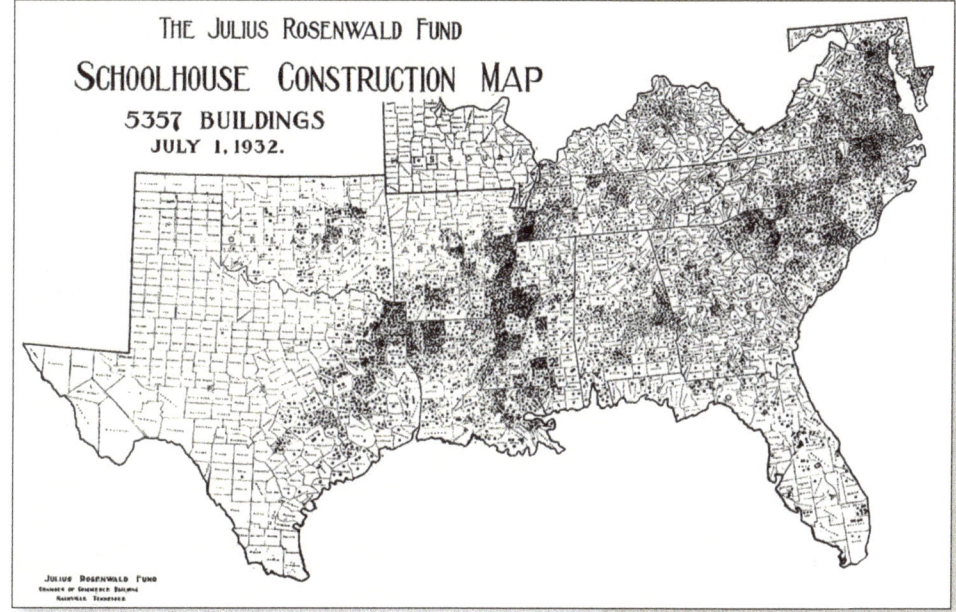

The Rosenwald Schools and Black Education in North Carolina

Nathan Carter Newbold, Director of Negro Education.
Photo courtesy of Duke University Archives

North Carolina Director of Negro Education Nathan Carter Newbold demonstrated considerable skill in convincing state legislators and local governments to allocate funds to match foundation grants for the construction of Rosenwald schools.

In 1913 the state appointed Nathan Carter Newbold the "Negro agent" for rural schools in North Carolina. A White man trained at Trinity College (later Duke University), Newbold had taught in Asheboro and Roxboro and worked as superintendent of schools in Washington County before being hired as Negro agent. He now made Black education his life's work, serving thirty-seven years in the same position.

Newbold's enthusiasm for Rosenwald schools predated formal creation of the fund. In 1915 Newbold arranged with Julius Rosenwald for the construction of one of the first schoolhouses outside the Tuskegee area. On October 8, 1915, the school—a two-teacher facility in Chowan County—was completed and inspected.

When the Rosenwald Fund was established in 1917, one of its first actions was to offer each state a grant to help hire a Black administrator to assist the White "Negro Agent." By 1918 Black assistants were at work with Director Newbold in North Carolina.[1]

NOTE: Nathan Carter Newbold's granddaughter, Margaret Newbold, Associate Director of Diversity for the Conservation Trust of North Carolina, has been an advocate and friend of the Mars Hill Anderson Rosenwald School, helping secure funds to reroof and save the old Mars Hill Rosenwald school building.

Our Story, This Place

Securing Funds to Build a Rosenwald School

Interest in securing Rosenwald Funds for Madison County came after investments in upgrading the older school building on Long Ridge in September 1925 for $300, plus labor and materials for around $100, and $250 for desks. The Madison County Board of Education requested that the Superintendent write the Rosenwald Fund for information relative to securing aid for the building of a Colored school at Mars Hill.[1]

Again in July of 1926, the Board directed the Superintendent to write the "Director of the Rosenwald Funds as to whether they would give assistance on a building with a site of less than two acres?"[2] By the middle of 1926, they reported "no action was taken on the Colored building at Mars Hill…"[3]

In the spring of 1927, C.M. Blankenship was elected as Superintendent of schools.[4] This same year, the Board purchased an additional acre of land from J.M. Rice for the Colored school site on Long Ridge,[5] and by July 1928, around $600 in funds were expended on a new Negro school building at Long Ridge.[6]

Superintendent Blankenship's correspondence to the Director of Rosenwald Funds explains that the Rosenwald Plan No. 20 was used in building the new Negro school house at Long Ridge; however, the Industrial Room was left off. "Can we still get Rosenwald Funds?"[7]

The Rosenwald monies for $750 came in the summer of 1929, and the first Rosenwald School class was taught at Long Ridge in 1929–1930.[8]

Ten years later, the Board of Education adopted the Rosenwald Community School Plan No. 6 for the White Madison County High School.[9]

The Rosenwald Community School Plans were used for many White school buildings in the South during the late 1930s and early 1940s, Madison County included.

Students and teacher at the Rosenwald A&M School, Tallahassee, Florida, 1923.
Photo courtesy of the University of Virginia Library

1930 Black School Enrollment in NC[10]

"Few Negroes in Madison"

According to the Feb. 7, 1930, issue of the *News Record,* "Madison County's total school enrolment is 83 Negro children, 9th smallest number of any in the state."

The numbers by county:

9	Mitchell County (smallest of all)
23	Clay County
46	Watauga County
47	Swain County
53	Cherokee County
61	Yancey County
75	Aleghany County
80	Avery County
83	Madison County

Those compared with 8,936 listed for Robeson County.

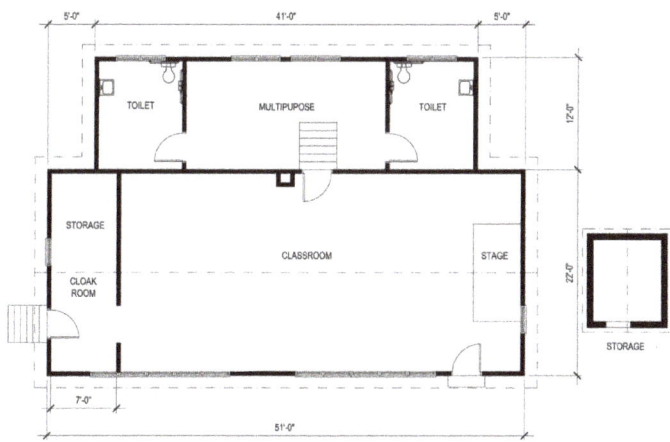

Updated floor plan for the school provided by Scott Donald, Padgett & Freeman Architects

The Historic Mars Hill Anderson Rosenwald School

Support from the Long Ridge Community

Parents and neighbors attending an event at the Long Ridge School.

Rosenwald Name[1]

Why did the Black school children not know that their school was a Rosenwald school building?

"Rosenwald always required financial buy-in from the Black community for building the schools. It would not have been equitable then to put his name on it. Also, Rosenwald may not have wanted to draw attention to a Jewish name on a building given the social exclusion of Jews during that period."

The Long Ridge School and Mt. Olive Baptist Church in Madison County had already manifested strong commitment to the community and to the education of their children. In 1925 they updated an older school for $300 plus $250 for desks, and approximately $100 for labor and materials. The building was still inadequate, but the members of the Long Ridge community had begun a tradition of community support in addressing the needs of local families.

In the spring of 1927 the Board of Education purchased an additional acre of land from J. M. Rice, and by July 1928 the community had raised approximately $600 toward construction of a new building on Long Ridge.

In correspondence with the Director of Rosenwald funds, the newly elected Superintendent, C. M. Blankenship, explained that Rosenwald Architectural Plan No. 20 had been used for the new school, which cost $2,093, except that the Industrial Room had been omitted. "Can we still get Rosenwald Funds," he asked. In response Rosenwald monies for $750 came in the summer of 1929, and that fall the first class was taught in the African American school, now known as the Mars Hill Anderson Rosenwald School.

How the Long Ridge Community Supported the School

Rosenwald funds for the school could not have been matched without the efforts of members of the Long Ridge community who contributed cash or in-kind labor and materials, wrote to the Superintendent of N.C. Schools, and lobbied the county school board and Board of Commissioners.

- Rosenwald Monies' Community Match
- Two Acres of Land Contributors
- School Road Builder
- Service of School Committee Persons
- Family Taxpayers
- School Census Takers
- Parents
  - Food Preparers, Lunch Boxes
  - Clothes Preparers
  - Special Programs Supporters
- Diggers of Water Line from Town to Community
- Transportation, Bus Drivers

- Community Participation in School Events
- Teachers
- Students
  - Mentors of Younger Students
  - Water Carriers
  - Coal Carriers
  - Kindling Makers
  - Fire Builders
  - Building Custodians
  - Groundskeepers
  - Grass Cutters

Madison County Black Community Families

African American children ages 6–21 in Madison County, North Carolina.

Federal Census 1930

MARS HILL:

Barnett, Oliver/Viola	6
Conley, Adeline	2
Coon, Doug/Sarah	2
Coon, Otis/Hattie	5
Elliot, Tilda	1
Hampton, Jim/Essie	5
Henson, John	5
Henson, Oscar/Zona	2
McDowell, Ullis/Dosha	3
Ray, Avery/Ida	4
Ray, Nate/Emma	5
Rooker, Clersie	3
Wilson, Ossie	2
Wilson, Sally	4
Young, Ruth	3

MIDDLE FORK:

Grifin, Tom/Effie E.	6
Ray, George/Laura L.	2

CALIFORNIA CREEK:

Briscoe, Gilbert/Fannie	8
Ray, Harve/Sarah	1
Ray, Nate/Mary	8
Wilson, John/Mary Ann	2

MARSHALL:

Baker, Hester	1
Barnett, Frank/Zora	4
Henry, Sarah	1
Jones, Mary	1
Jones, Will/Annie	3
McClain, Lena	2
Stokley, Lennard/Edna	3

HOT SPRINGS:

Atkins, Brazelton/Bell	2
Gudger, Issac S.	1
Henshaw, Blanch	3
Smith, Luther/Lurie	1

Total: 100

Federal Census 1940

MARS HILL:

Barnette, Oliver/Viola	4
Briscoe, Gilbert/Fanny	6
Briscoe, Umphrey/Tessie	1
Coones, Howard/Lena	2
Coones, Ottis/Hattie	2
Fergerson, Max/Velva	1
Hampton, Essie	1
Henson, Gaither/Ruby	3
McDowell, Dosky	5
Ray, Avery/Ida	5
Ray, John/Augusta	1
Ray, Nate/Mary	5
MH Roland, [Arseamous]/Mollie	4

MARS HILL continued:

Rutherford, James/Mary	2
Wells, H.A./Marie	1
Young, Oscar/Thelma	2

MARSHALL:

Jones, Hurbert	2
Stokley, Charlie/Maggie	4

HOT SPRINGS:

Houston, Blanch	2
Smith, Luther/Lucille	1
Stokley, Charlie/Maggie	4
Stokley, Mary	1
Walters, Tom/Minnie	6

Total: 67

Spelling of names used by census taker.

Is Your Family Name Listed?

Carry on the legacy by sharing your story, giving a donation, and telling others about this project.

The New Long Ridge Rosenwald School Building

The Long Ridge Rosenwald School began in the fall of 1929 and continued until 1959 when the school name was changed to Anderson Elementary School, to honor Joseph Anderson, the slave who went to prison one hundred years earlier, in 1859, for Mars Hill College's debt; that school name continued until integration in 1965.¹

In 1928, the Madison County School Board erected a new two-room school structure where the old building stood, using the Rosenwald School Plan No. 20, leaving the industrial room off the new building.² In 1929, $750 in monies came from the Rosenwald Fund of North Carolina and were matched by State, Madison County, and the Long Ridge Community monies.³

John Ferguson of the Long Ridge Community gave the $200 for the community match, according to oral tradition by Ms. Dorothy Coone of the community, school, and History Committee.⁴ Another acre of land was purchased in 1927, adjacent to the older school lot, from J.M. Rice and wife for $150.⁵ This additional land was required to secure Rosenwald funds for the new building, a Rosenwald requirement. Total cost for the school was $2,093.⁶

Eighty-three Negro children were enrolled in Madison County Colored schools in 1930 according to the North Carolina Superintendent of Public Instruction, "9th smallest of any county in the state."⁷

This beautiful new school building was a two-teacher school house that was intended to served all the Colored students of Madison County through the seventh grade.

The Long Ridge Rosenwald School, 1929–1959

Mary H. Wilson, teacher 1939-1953.
Photo courtesy of Fatimah´ Shabazz

The new two-room school house was built in 1928 on the old school site and qualified for Rosenwald Funds in 1929.[1]

The North Carolina Superintendent of Schools reported Madison County school houses in 1929–1930 as follows: five brick buildings; 48 frame buildings, 22 of which were one-room school buildings for White children; and two frame buildings, a one-room at Hot Springs, and the two-room at Mars Hill for "Colored" children.[2]

Black school-age-population possible enrollment dropped from over 150 in 1900 to 83 in 1930, with Marshall "Colored students" being bused to Mars Hill, starting in 1929.[3]

Mary H. Wilson was hired as teacher at the Rosenwald School in 1939 and she, with others from the community, met with the Madison County Board of Education, requesting improvements to the ten-year-old building: paint, underpin, water to the school, and a piano for the school. The Board of Education voted to improve the building and pay $10 down payment to Dunham's Music House for a piano. The school was to meet the remaining payments. Mrs. Wilson taught at the school for fourteen years, with Ms. M. Grace Owens as a second teacher during the last four years, 1949–1953.[4]

In 1959, the Board voted to ask Superintendent Fred W. Anderson to have the local school committee, Manuel Briscoe, Augusta Ray, and Seam Roland, "select an appropriate name for the Colored school. It was the feeling of the Board that an appropriate name would add prestige and dignity to the school."[5] The committee chose to rename the school Anderson Elementary, honoring Joseph Anderson who had helped in the founding of Mars Hill College.

M. Grace Owens, teacher 1949-1953

Mary Jane Katherine Haynes Wilson

Mrs. Mary H. Wilson attended Asheville City Schools. After graduating from Stephens-Lee High School, she went to Winston-Salem Teachers College, which was the first all-Black college to offer a degree in elementary education.[6] While there, she also obtained her Master's Degree in Music Appreciation. Later, she taught music classes in her Asheville home.

She taught for 16 years at the Long Ridge Anderson Colored School in Mars Hill, NC, 1938-1954, where she included music in her classroom along with the required educational classes.

Mrs. Wilson was married to Levie Wilson. Their daughter is Fatimah´ Rashida Shabazz, a.k.a. Beverly A. Wilson, Alumni Facilitator for the Mars Hill Anderson Rosenwald School.

It was Mr. Wilson who made the connection for Mrs. Wilson to the Long Ridge Colored School in Mars Hill. They were in need of a teacher, and she was in need of a job.[7]

> Many churches in Madison County were organized in the local school building.

Endnotes for Education and Rosenwald Schools

Madison County Community Schools, p. 16

1. John Angus McLeod, *From These Stones*, MHC.
2. Jinsie Underwood, *This Is Madison County*, 1975.
3. Hunter, *Education In Yancey County, NC*.
4. McLeod, p. 14.

Public Education in Madison County after the Civil War, p. 17

1. NC Annual Report of the Supt. of Public Instruction, June 30, 1874, p. 101.
2. Madison County Board of Education Minutes, 1896 (Office of County Commissioners, June 1, 1896), Sept. 1907.
3. Madison County School Expense Ledgers, MHU Archives, Local History, Box 103, Folder 2.
4. Minutes, June 5, 1905.
5. 1874 U.S. Civil Rights Bill, NC Annual Report of Sup't of Public Instruction, Nov. 1. 1874-75, pp. 63-64.

African American Public Education in Madison County, pp. 18-19

1. Madison County Board of Education Minutes, June 5, 1905.
2. MCBOE Minutes, April 27, 1965.
3. Madison County Board of Education "School Expense Ledger Book, 1901-1904" (Robert L. Moore, Superintendent) MHU Archives, Local History, Box 103, Folder 1.
4. Madison County Register of Deeds, Marshall, NC, Book 20, Page 186.
5. MCBOE Minutes, June 5, 1905, Microfilm, MHU Archives.
6. School Expense Ledger Book, 1903-1908, p. 151, MHU Archives, Local History, Box 103, Folder 2.
7. Richard Dillingham, "The Forks of Ivy," Unpublished Manuscript, 2013.
8. MCBOE Minutes, June 5, 1905.
9. Madison County Sentinel, "Mount Olive Church Might Have Record Breaking History," March 17, 1999, p. 14; Herbert Barnette Collection.
10. Madison County Heritage Book, Vol. I, p. 32.
11. David Hajou, *Lush Life: Biography of Billy Strayhorn*, p. 4 (New York: Farr, Straus Giroux) 1996.
12. Edwin B. Cheek, Interviews: Shirley Sewell; Augusta Ray; and Manuel Briscoe, 1983.
13. MCBOE Minutes, July 6, 1959.
14. Cheek, Sewell and Ray, 1983.
15. 1920 Federal Census, Madison County, NC.
16. 1905 Mars Hill Colored School Persons, Madison County Board of Education Minutes, 1905.

Julius Rosenwald, p. 20

1. Beverly Siegel, *From Sears to Eternity: The Julius Rosenwald Story*, 2002, WTTW, PBS, Chicago.
2. Peter Ascoli, *Schools of Hope: How Julius Rosenwald Helped Change African American Education*, Calkins Creek An Imprint of Highlights, 2014, Forward p. 8.
3. Peter Ascoli, *Julius Rosenwald: The Man Who Built Sears, Roebuck and Advanced the Cause of Black Education in the American South*, Philanthropic and Nonprofit Studies, 2006.

Booker T. Washington, p. 21

1. Wormser, Richard, *The Rise and Fall of Jim Crow*, Produced by Thirteen, WNET, New York, Educational Broadcasting System, 2002.
2. Norell, Robert J., *The Life of Booker T. Washington*, Harvard University Press, 2009.
3. Harlan, Louis R., *Booker T. Washington*, 2 vols. (1972, 1983), with Raymond W. Smock, eds., *The Booker T. Washington Papers*, 12 vols. (1972); August Meier, *Negro Thought in America, 1880-1915* (1963), University of North Carolina Press.
4. Steele, Shelby, *Pride and Compromise*, The New York Times, February 12, 2009.
5. Wormser, Richard, *The Rise and Fall of Jim Crow*, Produced by Thirteen, WNET, New York, 2002.

The Vision of Dr. Booker T. Washington & Mr. Julius Rosenwald, p. 22

1. "History of the Rosenwald School Program," National Trust for Historic Preservation, www.preservationnation.org

Overview of The Rosenwald Program, p. 23

1. *Investment in People: The Story of the Julius Rosenwald Fund*, Edwin R. Embree, 1949.

The Rosenwald Schools and Black Education in North Carolina, pg 24

1. Thomas W. Hanchett, "The Rosenwald Schools and Black Education in North Carolina," The North Carolina Historical Review, Volume LXV, Number 4, pp. 406-7, October, 1988.

Securing Funds to Build a Rosenwald School, p. 25

1. MCBOE Minutes, Nov. 2, 1925.
2. Ibid., July 5, 1926.
3. Ibid., July 19, 1926.
4. Ibid., April 13, 1927.
5. Ibid., July 5, 1927.
6. Ibid., July 9, 1928.
7. C.M. Blankenship Correspondence to Credle, Feb. 22, 1928, NC Archives.
8. Biennial Report of Supt. of Public Instruction of NC, Part III, 1929-1930, p. 314.
9. MCBOE Minutes, May 15, 1939.
10. 1930 Black School Enrollment in NC, The News Record, Feb. 7, 1930, p. 1; NC Superintendent of Public Instruction Report, 1930.

Booker T. Washington was considered the most influential Black educator of the late 19th and early 20th centuries.

> **In 1929, $750 in monies came from the Rosenwald Fund of North Carolina and were matched by State, Madison County, and the Long Ridge Community monies.**

Rosenwald Name, p. 26

1. Rosenwald Name, "A Critical Psycho-Biography of Kivie Kaplan Against The Backdrop of Black-Jewish Relations in the 20th Century," Steven Engel, American-Jewish Archives, Cincinnati, Ohio.

The New Long Ridge Rosenwald School Building, p. 28

1. Madison County Board of Education (MCBOE) Minutes, July 6, 1959. Extracted by Pauline Cheek and Dan Slagle.
2. Blankenship, Feb. 22, 1928.
3. Biennial Report, p. 314.
4. Oral Tradition by Dorothy Briscoe Coone, 2012.
5. MCBOE Minutes, July 5, 1927.
6. Fisk University, "Rosenwald Fund Card Database," Dan Slagle.
7. News Record, Marshall, NC, "Few Negroes in Madison," Feb. 7, 1930, p. 1.

The Long Ridge Rosenwald School, 1929–1959, p. 29

1. Biennial Report, p. 314.
2. 1900-1930 Federal Census, Madison County, NC; The News Record, Feb. 7, 1930, p. 1.
3. MCBOE Minutes, 1939-1953.
4. Madison County Heritage Book, Vol. I, p. 10.
5. Anderson Elementary School, Madison County History, MHU Archives.

Mary Jane Katherine Haynes Wilson, p. 29

6. MHC Hilltop Online, 2006: "A Teacher Remembers," Interview by Loretta Akins with Mrs. Wilson at age 93. (MHU and author, Reprint Permission Granted, 2021)
7. Input from the Wilson daughter, 2022.

Memories and Stories

A Visit from John D. Rockefeller, Jr.

John D. Rockefeller, Jr.

"We put on our Sunday-go-to-meeting clothes and wore them to school that day."

"I was born in 1913, and I started school when I was six; so that was 1919, and I finished the seventh grade, that's all that they had here. I was eight or nine years old when … John D. Rockefeller came through. I remember that the teacher told us to get dressed; so we put on our Sunday-go-to-meeting clothes and wore them to school that day. He had been to Marshall, so he came to Long Ridge School to see our work…

"So he came up—seems like it was a T-model Ford, he and two other guys. I know he had on a big Stetson-like hat, and I don't remember what the other people wore, 'cause all we wanted to see was the richest man in the world, John D. Rockefeller. So we saw him… He appropriated the money for us to add an addition to the school, and this additional room was called the John D. Rockefeller Room."

From an interview with Mrs. Shirley [Barnette] Sewell, conducted June 9, 1983 by Edwin Cheek.

Arts and Crafts in the Long Ridge School

Shirley (Barnette) Sewell

I will be seventy years old on June 27, 1983. I started school at Long Ridge at age six and finished the seventh grade. Our teacher, Mrs. Fortune, from Old Fort, taught us to make shuck dolls, whisk brooms, and pottery. We'd take a certain kind of red clay from the bank near the school, get it wet till we could work it good, and shape it any way we wanted. We'd put it on racks, two layers with bricks to hold the heat, and then build a fire. It was just a one-room school, so we had to make it outside.

At special events our parents would come and look at our pottery. Some would buy it. Mrs. Fortune was real good at all different crafts. We made shuck rugs, picture frames; we took pictures from magazines and folded them to make pretty belts. With clay we made jugs, vases, large, small, even water pitchers. As good as any you buy in a store. People from Mars Hill College and everywhere came to buy them. It was something to see.

Shirley Sewell, daughter of Viola King Barnette.
Photo courtesy of Charity Ray

Augusta (Briscoe) Ray

I went to Long Ridge School about 1924 and finished out the seventh grade. We made pottery about 1927 or '28. Ruby Fortune was our teacher… This here red clay, it looks right slick. We got it out back from the school, and we rolled it out by hand, then baked it… We made corn shuck dolls and shuck mats, and other things from shucks; I can remember John D. Rockefeller coming to visit Long Ridge. We had the pottery on show for him, our parents and people of the community.

Manuel Briscoe

I started at Long Ridge School in 1927, and we made pottery about 1930. Our teacher was Charity Hazard, from Abingdon, Virginia… She made us get buckets of clay near a small branch below the school… We'd get a vase or bowl formed and then work it down to make it smooth inside and out. Then we'd set it out to dry. We did not fire it in a kiln. When it was dry we'd paint it. We took our pottery to the fair in Asheville in the fall of the year… We'd take baskets made out of walnuts and crossbows and arrows. One fellow won a shotgun with his crossbow. I won a blue ribbon, surprisingly enough.

Augusta Briscoe Ray
Photo courtesy of Charity Ray

Alumni interviews conducted in 1983 by Edwin B. Cheek

The Water Story on Long Ridge

Each day buckets of water were carried by the older students from the bottom of the hill below the school and placed on the school water shelf where a dipper hung for the students.

Open springs were available in the valleys on both sides of Long Ridge, west on Long Ridge Road in the hollow above the John Ammons home place, or east on what became South Main Street, near the Robel West home place.

Therefore, when Madison County Board of Education built the new Mars Hill Colored School on Long Ridge in 1905, buckets of water were carried by the older students from the bottom of the hill below the school, from a spring beside South Main Street. Fresh buckets of water were placed on the school water shelf daily where a dipper hung for the students. This system continued until in the 1930s when students became sick through contaminated water from open springs.

Manuel Briscoe described this sad event during an interview with Pauline Cheek, years later, in 1984: "It took the deaths of three Black children from typhoid fever before an agreement could be reached whereby Blacks furnished the labor and Whites the lines to take water to the Black Long Ridge Community."[1]

Seemingly, the matter was complicated because the Long Ridge Community was outside the town limits for water service, but the two groups worked together and solved the problem.

Extending the Town of Mars Hill water line to the Long Ridge Community still required that students carry buckets of water a long distance, "approximately 2,000 feet"[2] to the school, that is, almost as far as Mt. Olive Church.

It was in the mid-1940s before the water line was extended to the school[3] house. That gave the school children an outside water spigot.[4]

Only in the 1950s did the school house get inside plumbing and restrooms.

Black Folkways in Madison County: Doctors[1]

"Up until the 1930s and 1940s, most Black people in Madison County had never been to a doctor for any of their medical problems. Black women doctored their children with roots and teas. When they had their children they used the services of the local midwife, Aunt Tillie Elliot. She charged around six dollars to deliver a baby, but Dr. Locke, the White doctor, charged fifteen dollars. The midwife delivered babies for both Blacks and Whites."

~ *Charlene Delores Ray*

Black Home Remedies of the Briscoes

We went barefoot as kids. We'd stump a toe—it would be nearly hangin' off—but the doctor'd get pine rosin and bind it up and first thing you knew it would be healed.

We'd bring in resin and steep it and make a tea for colds. We'd put in on sores and on horses when the bridle rubbed them. We raised Rhode Island Reds and Plymouth hens, and we'd dye their eggs—brown with walnuts and gold with sage. We made real good wine back then—blackberry and grape. Some people used yeast, but we just put in sugar and let it work till it quit. Wine helps cramps.

We collected all sorts of wild stuff—poke, plantain, thistle (it was thorny), wild mustard, lamb's quarters. Sumac tea was good for bed-wetters. We'd decorate with galax wreaths. Gudger Barnett would kill a hog and his wife would render out the fat for people to take with a little sugar at night, like cod liver oil. Blacks and Whites both came for that. Also onion plasters were used. We'd cut pumpkins like wheels and hang them on a hoe handle to dry for food.

My daddy kept the [branch] banks grubbed. He knew how to keep things fixed. If the wind blew wooden shingles off something like the chicken coop he'd make new ones out of oak wood, and they would stay on. He made oak-bottomed chairs, and he got hickory splits to tie chair bottoms. The Blacks, that was their thing. We got broom straw to make brooms; the kids scraped off the seeds for it. My uncle made split baskets, and White folks bought them. A lady on Middle Fork made them. Charity Ray has a picture of one of the baskets. I remember Aunt Sarah with a basket full of goodies. Some baskets were square, and there was a gizzard basket. My mother knit little booties and sweaters and quilted. We'd have quilting parties.

My mother used horse mint for bronchitis. Boneset was bitter stuff, but you would boil it and drink it for a cough. For nerves you'd boil catnip and drink it at night. We'd boil wintergreen and make a syrup for coughs. I keep it and take it with a little brown sugar. It's hard to find good molasses now. My daddy made it the old way; and oh boy, that was good. He raised everything we ate, even wheat, peanuts, rutabagas, all that stuff in our garden. He and mother pickled cucumbers and made kraut in a wooden keg. He raised celery. My mother would take tansy for the blood in spring. We'd make spice wood tea, sweeten it and drink it cold or hot. My mother used to take molasses and sulfur to purify the blood, and I'd try it once in a while.

"My mother would take tansy and wash it real good, cut it and put it in a jar, and we'd drink it. White plantain was good for women's discharge. My mother-in-law, Doskey McDowell, would cut it up and make a drink out of it.

"Sassafras tea was good for the blood in spring. We'd make spice wood tea, sweeten it and drink it cold or hot. I had whooping cough one time. A neighbor had a mare so daddy went to him and got some mare's milk, and it cured my cough. A lot of people used mare's milk."

Interview with Manuel Briscoe by Pauline and Edwin B. Cheek, 1983

> "For nerves you'd boil catnip and drink it at night. We'd boil wintergreen and make a syrup for coughs."

Hands-on Learning Had Long Roots

Manuel Briscoe

Chair, MHARS Committee, 1960–1964

Interviewed June 18, 1983

Johnny Ray & Margaret Barnette, Manuel Briscoe & Frances McDowell.
Photo courtesy of Charity Ray

For the fair we made pitchers, vases, and bowls and painted them with watercolors. Also we made a type of basket with a handle and carved birds—ducks and other type of fowl.

I started at Long Ridge School in 1927, and we made pottery about 1930. Our teacher was Charity Hazard from Abingdon, Virginia. I don't know where she learned pottery, but when she came, she really knew how to do the job. She made us get buckets of clay near a small branch below the school. We didn't mix anything with it. If it was too soft, we'd let it dry till we could knead it like flour [dough], stiff enough to roll out to form a base. We'd take a little water on a knife or paddle to smooth it.

We'd get a vase or bowl formed and then work it down to make it smooth inside and out. Then we'd set it out to dry. We did not fire it in a kiln. When it was dry we'd paint it. Charity Hazard was craft-minded, and we took our pottery to the fair in Asheville in the fall of the year. In those days, we'd take baskets [carved] out of walnuts and crossbows [with] arrows. One fellow won a shotgun with his crossbow. I won a blue ribbon, surprisingly enough.

A Pearson fellow was head of the fair for Blacks, held on a vacant lot on the corner of McDowell and Southside. Charity taught at Long Ridge for two years and then went to Burnsville. [Student] Hugh Lee Griffin; I knew him well. I was talking with Charles Young today, and he said Charity Hazard taught crafts there. She passed less than a year ago in Richmond, and her husband burned up in an accident in a house.

For the fair we made pitchers, vases, and bowls and painted them with watercolors. Also we made a type of basket with a handle and carved birds – ducks and other type of fowl. You know, in those days we called that junk, but now we value it. I doubt that you could find anybody who kept any. Under the school building there's two feet of coal dust; I doubt whether you could find any pieces of pottery.

Mr. Briscoe tried to recall names of teachers at Long Ridge. His first teacher was…Mackie. His second teacher was Mrs. Roseberry. Other names he mentioned were Mrs. Phillips from Lenoir, Mrs. Davis, and Mrs. Conley. "Our teacher trusted me and another boy to take her check, about $50 a month, to the bank."

Interview by Pauline and Edwin B. Cheek, 1983

Augusta Ray

Mother of Charity Ray and Dorothy Coone

Interviewed June 15, 1983

My mother was born on September 17, 1893, in Yancey County, and my daddy in Madison County. I was born on Paint Fork in Madison County, the oldest of 14 children. I married when I was [nineteen]. I went to Long Ridge School about 1924 and finished out the seventh grade.

We made pottery about 1927 or 28. Ruby Fortune was our teacher. I don't know where she was from. She was married. She taught two or three years. You had to have water to make the pottery. This here red clay, it looks right slick. We got it out back from the school, and we rolled it out by hand, then baked it. I don't remember any glaze. We made corn shuck dolls and shuck mats, and other things from shucks. I can kind-of remember John D. Rockefeller coming to visit Long Ridge. We had the pottery on show for parents and people of the community.

I have one of the teachers' pictures, Sallie Ledbetter Davidson, who taught my second year. She was born May 19, 1895, to William and Anna Logan Ledbetter and graduated from Johnson C. Smith University. We went to see her in a Charlotte convalescent home on September 17, 1977. We were so proud to see her, and she was proud to see us, too.

Daddy played the guitar—religious songs and the old-timey hoedowns. John Hanson, my mother's daddy, played fiddle for both Whites and Blacks. They'd play long into the night. Mother did the cooking, and Daddy would call all the children around for prayers. We sat around a square wooden table, and he would say thanks. I enjoyed being with other children in the community. Oh yes, we'd walk to school; there was no other way. When I finished Long Ridge, I went to work for Dr. Willard Robinson—cooking and house work. I'd read to little baby Ray—"Little Red Hen," and "The Sky Is Falling," and "The Three Little Pigs." Daddy was wanting to send me to Johnson City to his sister's so I could go to school, but you had to have clothes. He was share-cropping, and he had to work hard. He had to clear off a field, go in and grub it. He'd start in the fall of the year to burn brush, and then he'd plow for summer. It was hard work.

Interview by Pauline and Edwin B. Cheek, 1983

Augusta Briscoe Ray attended the Long Ridge Colored School and served on the school committee, 1953-1965.
Photo courtesy of daughter Charity Ray

The Historic Mars Hill Anderson Rosenwald School

Viola King Barnette Writes a Letter[1]

Viola King Barnette was a washerwoman for Mars Hill College personnel. All of her children, including Shirley Sewell, attended Long Ridge School that went to the seventh grade.

Mrs. Barnette wrote to the Superintendent of NC Schools saying that her children and other rural children were not able to attend high school and keep the new law requiring that all NC children attend school until age sixteen, as rural high schools do not exist in many rural counties such as Madison County.

In response she was told that because of her letter, all children in NC would have access to secondary education. Thus busing began for Madison County Colored students to Stephens-Lee High School in Asheville, and continued until integration in 1965.

Viola King Barnette's story is told by Emily Wilson in *Hope and Dignity: Older Black Women of the South*.

Viola Barnette, Crusader for Black Education[2]

Viola King Barnette was a crusader for Black education who became acutely aware of the unfairness of an educational system that required all students to attend school until they turned 16, but refused to provide high schools for rural Black students.

Under segregation in the 1940s, African American children were barred from the White schools, and in Madison County there was no Black high school; all-Black Long Ridge School went only from first through seventh grade. As a result, when students finished at the Long Ridge School (later the Joe Anderson School) in Mars Hill, or any other Black school in the county, they were required to repeat seventh grade over and over until they turned 16. Their only other option was to attend the segregated Stephens-Lee High School in Asheville, but the state did not take responsibility for transporting students to high school.

With some help from Caroline and Martha Biggers, teachers at Mars Hill College, and from Cornelia Vann, for whom Mrs. Barnette did washing, her daughter Shirley was sent to boarding school for a year. She got a job as cook to help pay her tuition. Her sister Blanch and brother David spent the week with her in Asheville in order to attend Stephens-Lee.

Like her children, most of Viola King Barnette's grandchildren have fulfilled her vision of the importance of education, continuing on to college and graduate school, earning masters and doctorates, and some working at colleges themselves. One grandchild, a PhD, is on the staff of Central College in Durham, North Carolina. Her grandson Kevin Barnette, Mars Hill University's Assistant Football Coach, describes her this way.

"I never saw her frustrated. She never raised her voice. She always knew it was going to happen. She was the most positive person I've ever been around. She just believed God was going to work it out. She always smiled. She sang all the time, and she spoke in the softest voice."

True to her favorite hymn, "I'm on the Battlefield," Viola Barnette spoke out for a better education for African American children in Madison County when no one else shared her hope.

"It never made sense to her that they just would continue to repeat the same grade," Coach Barnette recalled during an interview with the Hilltop staff. "My grandmother wasn't a person to really show a lot of emotions, but she thought that was pretty stupid."

Emily Herring Wilson described Viola Barnette's reaction in her 1983 book, *When the Sun Goes Down*, about the influence of elderly Black women.

"She'd 'ask around' if there was any way buses could take the children from Mars Hill and other small villages into Asheville, 25 miles away, where they could advance through high school…

In frustration, Mrs. Barnette wrote to the NC Superintendent of Schools asking that something be done about the problem. She ultimately received a letter from him, informing her that buses would be made available to take them to Stephens-Lee—an hour each way. The superintendent wrote, "Because of your interest in this matter, in the future all North Carolina children, Black and White, will have a chance to go to high school."

Mrs. Barnette, who died in 1983 at the age of 91, was honored during Martin Luther King Day ceremonies at Mars Hill College in 2006 "for her contribution toward equal secondary education opportunities for all children in North Carolina."

Coach Barnette said his grandmother would not take any credit for her accomplishment were she alive today. "I know for a fact she would give God all the glory."

A Mars Hill graduate himself, Kevin was reared in Madison County and still lives here today with his family. His fondest memory of his grandmother is that she loved kids, and that she would treat them with great respect.

"She'd get down to your level and talk to you… She always had toys in her house for kids. Even up into her eighties she would be on the floor playing with kids. Everything had a rhyme or reason to it. It either had a learning concept to it, or a spiritual concept. She never wasted her words. When she said something, it always had unbelievable substance to it."

She stressed education and wanted all her children to go to school to get an education and be successful. "She wanted them to desire to have an education."

He said the first time he understood the wide impact of his grandmother was in 1997, when he was flown to Duke University Hospital in Durham for emergency heart surgery. I had two heart surgeries at Duke, and I was in the heart tower. One day I was walking and a gentleman came into my room. I didn't know him from Adam. He said he was Robert Seymour."

Viola King Barnett.
Photo: Susan Mullallay

He learned later that Robert Seymour is a well-known pastor in the Chapel Hill area who during the days of segregation was influential in fighting to integrate churches, restaurants, and schools in that area. Early in his career he had been pastor at Mars Hill Baptist Church. Viola Barnette had worked for him. "He told me during that time that my grandmother played a real important role in how he saw Civil Rights and his spiritual walk during the time that she worked for him. And to me that was really amazing. Finding out and knowing who Robert Seymour is, and finding out and knowing that she had that big an impact."

She supported Martin Luther King and other Civil Rights leaders. She despised racism so much that she had her name changed from Barnett to Barnette with an "e" on the end because the governor of Mississippi at the time (Ross Barnett) had the same name and she loathed the things he did to defend segregation. "It's very important to me when people write my name that it has an "e" on the end," said Coach Barnette.

Many years after the first buses took children from Madison County into Asheville to school, Madison County public schools finally opened their doors to Black students.

Coach Barnette, who went to school in the early 1970s, had five older brothers. "I know that four of my brothers had a hard time with integration. Once they got into high school, all four of them said there's no way we're going to go through that. They all went into some service, Army, Navy…

Black Politics in Madison County[1]

"None of the Blacks interviewed had been voting all their lives. The earliest recorded date that anyone could remember voting was 1940. Most of the people remembered their grandparents or parents who had voted, always voted Republican… However, the old affiliation to the Republican Party has died out.

There was only one 'die-hard Republican' out of all the Blacks interviewed. Most of the Blacks now vote for the person who they think will do a better job. More likely that person will be a Democrat."

~ *Charlene Delores Ray*

His own experience in Madison County's newly integrated schools was positive.

"By the time I got there, it was so much easier. All my friends that I grew up with, we all went to the elementary school here. From here I went to high school. I played Little League baseball. Little League football. I was involved in the Boy Scouts, the Cub Scouts, and all those things with all those kids from the time I was very young.

"I haven't had any racial problems in Madison County. I know that sounds impossible, but I haven't. I grew up and basically spent my entire life here."

He was then and is now continually inspired by his grandmother's persistence and faith. "Her walking a mile and a half carrying clothes and washing people's clothes, and taking care of nine children by herself… I have it easy compared with that! She saw through her spiritual walk that all things were possible."

Kevin Barnette

This profile was adapted from "Viola Barnette: Spoke Out for Education," with permission from Mars Hill University's The Hilltop Online *student newspaper, January 23, 2006. Interview and story development by Loretta Akins, Joseph Ayers, Shatara Drummond, Rachel Dudley, Chris Hewitt, Xavier Jordan, Katie Powell, Matt Welch, Ryan Wright, and Deidre Abouahmed.*

Shirley Sewell

Daughter of Viola King Barnette

Interviewed June 9, 1983

I will be seventy years old on June 27, 1983. I started school at Long Ridge at the age of six and finished the seventh grade. Our teacher, Mrs. Fortune, from Old Fort, taught us to make shuck dolls, whiskbrooms, and pottery. We'd take a certain kind of red clay from the bank near the school, get it wet till we could work it good and shape it any way we wanted. We'd put it on racks, two layers with bricks to hold the heat, and then build a fire. It was just a one-room school; so we had to make it outside. At special events our parents would come and look at our pottery. Some would buy it.

Mrs. Fortune was real good at all different crafts. We made shuck rugs, picture frames; we took pictures from magazines and folded them to make pretty belts. With clay we make jugs, vases, large, small, even water pitchers. As good as any you buy in a store. People from Mars Hill College and everywhere came to buy them. It was something to see.

John D. Rockefeller came to visit Long Ridge School, and we had an "exhibition" for him. We had pottery on display, and also we took pretty flowers. The teacher told all of us to get dressed up. It was like an outing. We carried our lunch and baked a cake. We were told he was the richest man in the world, and we were going to see him. He came in a Model-T Ford and wore a Stetson-like hat. He stayed a couple of hours. He was impressed with the rugs, and more so with the pottery. He got some. He appropriated money for a new room. I was eight or nine when he came. I graduated in 1929, and the second room was built in 1927. Miss Luck and Miss Davis were my last teachers. They would take time with you and tell you how to look forward to the future.

Edwin B. Cheek in 1983

NOTE: Interviews were by Edwin B. Cheek, son of Dr. Edwin R. Cheek, and Pauline Binkley Cheek, in a 1983 summer internship for credit at Mars Hill College, while a student at Wake Forest College. His research was "Arts and Crafts at Long Ridge School," supervised by Richard Dillingham.

> "Daddy played the guitar—religious songs and the old-timey hoedowns."

Shirley Sewell.
Photo courtesy of Charity Ray

> We'd take a certain kind of red clay from the bank near the school and make jugs, vases, large, small, even water pitchers. At special events our parents would come and look at our pottery.

The Historic Mars Hill Anderson Rosenwald School

Flora "Flo" Young Barnette

Herbert and Flo Barnette

Granddaughter of James Coleman Young and Martha M. Young

Grandfather James was son of Marcus Young and Fannie Gurley

Grandmother Martha was daughter of Caroline and Peter Young[1]

Sister of brother Melvin Young of Long Ridge

Wife of Herbert Barnette (deceased), who was the son of Viola King Barnette

Their home was on Long Ridge

Mother of Larry; Jerry; with Dennis and David Carson on Long Ridge

by Herbert: Gregory (deceased), and Kevin Barnette of Mars Hill

Flo has family memories of three different families connected to the Long Ridge Community: her and Herbert's family; her Young grandparents who raised her and her brother in Spruce Pine, NC; and her mother-in-law Viola King Barnette of Gabriel's Creek at Mars Hill.

Flo met her future husband Herbert when visiting her grandmother Clarisse Rucker Wilson, mother of Howard Rucker, at Mount Olive Baptist Church. She and Herbert reared their blended families in the Long Ridge Community.

Her childhood food memories from her grandparents' meals were typical of older mountain families. Breakfast consisted of sausage, bacon, or ham, poached eggs with gravy, and hot biscuits with fresh cow's milk and butter. Other meals consisted of vegetables, corn, beans, potatoes, pork, chicken, or wild meats (bird, rabbit, squirrel, fish) with creasy or poke salad greens in Spring, with turnip and collard greens in the Fall, always with hot cornbread, occasionally having hot apple or berry-cobbler pie for desert.

The Young grandchildren always helped to produce and harvest the garden. Flo's younger brother's help was limited because of his having polio. Hands-on gardening gave lasting memories of the "best-tasting foods possible" for their hungry, young, growing bodies. Also, in the fall of the year, they participated in the food harvest and preservation by canning vegetables in the big cannery. After slaughtering the hog, they would salt the meat for storing in the smoke house above the root cellar, where the salted hams hung for curing. They helped pickle the beans and cabbage sauerkraut with salt brine in crockpots, or helping string up the green beans to dry for "leather britches." She fondly remembers how they preserved their turnips and cabbage underground in the garden. By digging two pits, one for turnips and one for cabbage, placing the cabbage, roots turned up, covered with dry grass and earth, until one big head would be removed during winter, for "the sweetest tasting cabbage possible." They harvested bushels of apples and potatoes for storing in the root cellar, where they also preserved their onions.

Flo remembers helping her grandmother Young do laundry, building the fire under the big, black, wash-pot of water, adding the lye soap, using the scrub board, rinsing the clothes, and hanging them on the clothesline to dry; even ironing some of the clothes with the flat irons, heated in front of the fire at the fireplace. This training helped prepare her for helping her future mother-in-law iron shirts and blouses for White families in Mars Hill for added family income.

Two favorite events of the week were going to school and church. After attending their Black elementary school in Spruce Pine, they traveled by a small bus to Hudson High School in Marion, NC. Little did she know that her future mother-in-law Viola King Barnette was responsible for her access to high school,[2] as was her future husband Herbert who had attended the elementary school on Long Ridge and high school in Asheville, NC, riding the public bus from Mars Hill to Lexington Avenue, then walking the long mile distance to Stephens-Lee High School.[3]

Going to church on Sunday was a full day's event. They had Sunday school and preaching in the morning with singing and fellowship, and an evening service with more worship and Christian fellowship. Both grandparents were religious, "teaching us values that have served us well for life."[4]

Memories of Family, Community, and School

Dedicated to the descendants of Sarah Roland Weston Hart

Sarah Roland's family moved to Madison County and the Long Ridge Community in 1939. The Rolands, her father's family, came from Higgins in Yancey County. Her mother Mollie Carson's family was from Bakersville, NC. Sarah was born on Long Ridge in August of the same year, and admits that she may have been spoiled, being the youngest in the family, as her work chores were less than those of her older siblings.

The Rolands grew up on Higgins Branch in west Yancey County; Sarah's father was one out of ten children. For three generations they had owned their farms, homes, and the church, which is the location of the Roland Graveyard. Grandmother Kizzie Roland, a Blackfoot Indian, shared her knowledge of wild plants and herbs for medicinal purposes with the Rolands. She would prepare a liquid tonic from budded peach twigs for breaking fever; "horrible taste, but it worked!"

Mother Mollie Carson grew up in Bakersville, NC, and her mother Sarah Forney's family was from West Virginia, for whom her great-granddaughter Sarah would be named.

Father Arseamous was able to buy numerous acres of land in the Mars Hill area: on Mt. Olive Drive, Long Ridge Road, and out on Woods Ammons Drive, beyond where the JW Church would be built, including the future John and Augusta Ray property. By this time, eighteen Black families had settled in the Long Ridge Community, according to the 1940 Federal Census, where Arseamous was listed as a farmer.

Also, that census lists five Long Ridge Community men as employed by the former CCC Camp Joe, as Works Progress Administration (WPA) workers: Howard Coon, Vern Ray, June McDowell, Avery Ray, and a CCC youth, Fred Fegurson,[1] replacing the CCC boys who entered WW II. Camp Joe was located on Mars Hill's South Main Street, near the Long Ridge Community. It was a Tennessee Valley Authority Conservation Camp, named for Joseph Anderson.[2] The WPA workers continued the CCC conservation work in the area, setting White Pines, wire-staking washed-out gullies, and building privies in the area.

Sarah's memories of her family, community, and school are still fresh and rewarding. The family joined the Mt. Olive Baptist Church, and Sarah's three school-age siblings were enrolled in the Long Ridge Colored School nearby.

Her father became a Deacon in the church and a member of the Long Ridge School Committee.

All family members were expected to be seated at the table for meals, where father said the blessing: "In Jesus' name we pray, Amen." The Roland farm produced most of the food for the family table. All families were "seed savers," planting in the spring, after freezing weather had passed.

That farm supplied corn, wheat, and oat grains for flour, and meal for breads and animal feed. Dad would have his grains ground into meal or flour at the Fork's water-powered grist mill. Sugar cane was grown for making sorghum molasses. Dad had one horse, one mule, two cows for milk and butter, two sheep for sheared wool, hogs for meat, with a flock of chickens for meat and eggs.

Sarah Roland Weston Hart

Father: Arseamous "Seam" Roland. His parents: James Roland & Kizzie Morgan Roland, Blackfoot Indian

Mother: Mollie Carson Roland. Her parents: George Carson & Sarah Forney Carson

Siblings: (Yancey) Kathleen, Cecil, Kermit [early deaths] Edna, Kenneth, Sherrell, Geraldine

Children: Robbie Weston (daughter), Oscar Weston, Cecil Weston, Randall Weston, Stevie Weston. Father: James Weston

Descendants: 23 grandchildren; 50 great-grandchildren; 12 great-great-grandchildren[3]

The Ray and Roland Grocery Store was located beside Long Ridge Road, across from the church property. His partner was neighbor Avery Ray. They sold flour, meal, sugar, drinks, and candy.

The garden produced green cornfield and bush beans, Irish and sweet potatoes, beets, onions, tomatoes, peas, carrots, squash, cucumbers, okra, cabbage, rhubarb, turnips and greens, collard, spinach, kale, and mustard greens, and tame strawberries. In the orchard were two apple trees (Yellow Delicious and Sheep-Nose), two grapevines, a peach tree, a cherry tree, and a chestnut tree.

Wild foods in the spring included creasy greens, dandelion greens, and poke salad. Some nights we had crackling cornbread and Spice Wood tea for supper. The children helped gather and pick the wild foods in the fall: artichokes, persimmons, blackberries, chinquapins (dwarf chestnuts), hazelnuts, and black walnuts.

Our burley tobacco crop supplied the major income in our family. Burley tobacco came to the WNC Mountains in the 1930s. When our family's crop sold at Asheville in November or December, that major income brought rewards to all concerned: Daddy's car, though "I was nervous to ride with him, early on;" Mother's wringer washing machine, "even if we had to help pull some of the clothes through the wringer" for hanging on the clothesline to dry; a piano into our musical family; and new shoes and clothes, each fall, for growing and proud children.

The Rolands were a musical family. Father and Mother were the first family to own a piano on Long Ridge. Her brother Sherrell had a strong and beautiful voice.

Brother Kenneth played the harmonica, Granddaddy James Roland played the guitar, and Aunt Effie Roland Griffin played the banjo and was a good buck dancer, even when barefooted. Her son Oscar and siblings are all musical, singing in the church and have a band called Westsound. Sarah claims music from the hour of her birth, when Dr. Lock Robinson came to the house and assisted with her birthing. When Sarah was born, so they say, Dr. Lock began singing his celebration ditty: "Just Mollie and Me and the Baby make three."

Even though Dad only had a fourth-grade education, he became a good tobacco farm manager, and a shrewd business man in operating the Ray and Roland Grocery Store, located beside Long Ridge Road, across from the church property. His partner was neighbor Avery Ray. They sold flour, meal, sugar, drinks, and candy. Dad kept a daily store ledger, listing customers who bought on credit and made their payments, as well as all store bills.

After the crops were laid-by, the church held the annual revival, which would last a week. Those converted would be baptized into church membership. Sarah became a Christian when she was twelve. Their baptizing followed the revival on Sunday afternoon in the river at the Forks of Ivy. Sarah remembers that the church met by the stream at the Tom Willis place, singing and praying, then the baptizing. In the river stream with the first to be baptized, the Rev. Smith raised his hand in prayer and prayed: "I baptize you in the name of the Father, Son, and Holy Spirit," placing the candidate under water, back down with head up stream, after which, the Rev. Smith, said "Amen," and the congregation applauded. The youth were very familiar with this river, having played in the water many times before, except when "seeing a snake in the stream!"

Two of Sarah's memories are of Funerals and Decoration of the Graves. At funerals, the Holcombe Funeral Home would be in charge of preparing the corpse, the coffin, and grave. The women of the community would prepare food for the bereaved family. The men would sit-up with the corpse during the night. The church would help lay the loved one to rest the next day.

Decoration Day was held in the fall of the year, after the crops had been harvested. For the Roland family's grave decoration on Higgins Branch, Seam Roland, with other men, would go to the graveyard the week before and clean the graves, rounding each grave with soil, in preparation for the fresh flowers. Family members would bring food and baked goods for dinner-on-the-ground, especially Aunt Lena's baked apple pies. After lunch, there would be grave decoration with fresh flowers, then worship with singing, prayers, and testimonials, concluding with fellowship with many relatives from various states, saying: "good-by, until we meet again!"

Big Fall events for the family and community were hog-killing time and making molasses. Daddy had a molasses boiler and a cane juice press. The cane juice stalks would be cut and fodder removed, saving the seed heads for feeding the chickens, and seed for the next years' cane crop. With the horse "Bonnie" circling the press, the cane stalks were fed into the press, filling the barrel with cane juice. The boiler was a large metal pan, maybe two feet wide and six feet long, and about four inches deep. It had long wood sidebars, longer than the pan, giving handles on both ends of the boiler to lift the cane juice onto the furnace. The wood furnace had two low rock walls on either side to hold the boiler for the cooking. It would take more than two hours to boil down the five to ten gallons of cane juice into thick molasses, having to be skimmed constantly to remove the foam.

The children were not allowed near the hot molasses making. When the boiling molasses reached the drip test, the pan of thick molasses was lifted off the furnace fire and poured into three-gallon crocks for storing. Then, the children were allowed to sop the boiler, using pieces of cane stalk. Other families in the community were allowed to use the Roland cane-press and boiler, paying a small barter amount for usage.

The fat hogs were shot, then scalded in a barrel of boiling water for scraping the hair, then hung up for butchering. All parts of the hog were saved and used for chitterlings, cracklings, brains, hogs' feet, bacon, fatback, shoulders, and hams. The fatback would be salted for preservation, while bacon, shoulders, and hams would be smoked and hung in the smoke house. The sausage would be ground and cooked for canning. Hog killing took more than just a day to preserve the most important meat source for the family. "The sliced baked shoulder was the best!"

Some of Sarah's best memories are from her school days on Long Ridge. Her teachers were Mrs. Wilson, Ms. Best, and Ms. Owens. They always began the school day with both classes for devotion with scripture, prayer, and singing. Further, the older children were required to memorize scriptures: Psalms 23; Romans 12; and others. They were also taught Black History, "The Three Bs of Black Education: Mary McLeod Bethune; Charlotte Hawkins Brown; and Nannie Burroughs. For lunch, the children returned home in the community, while others carried their lunch. Games during their breaks would be on the playground beside the school. One favorite game was the big circle game Duck-Duck-Goose. The Goose would tag a Duck, and the Duck must chase and catch the Goose, or become the Goose themselves! The favorite event during the year was graduation. The students got to do the Big Circle Dance, where boys and girls got to circle together, "the girls wearing their long white dresses!"[4]

After graduation, Sarah attended Stephens-Lee High School, then Mars Hill College, the first Black from Long Ridge and Madison County to graduate from the college.[5] Sarah taught school in Asheville, NC and in VA, where she received her Masters' Degree from George Mason University. Retiring back in Asheville, Sarah joined the Friends Group for rehabilitating her Mars Hill Anderson Rosenwald School, where she serves on its History Committee.

> **Some of Sarah's best memories are from her school days on Long Ridge. They always began the school day with both classes for devotion with scripture, prayer, and singing. They were also taught Black History, "The Three Bs of Black Education: Mary McLeod Bethune; Charlotte Hawkins Brown; and Nannie Burroughs.**

The Historic Mars Hill Anderson Rosenwald School

A Teacher Remembers

by Loretta Atkins, from the Hilltop, *the student newspaper of Mars Hill College, 2008*

At the age of 93, Mary Wilson has felt the winds of change blow and has seen all the differences that came as a result.

Wilson, who once taught at the Long Ridge/Anderson School, was born in 1913 and is "just trying to make 100!"

She attended Asheville city schools. After graduating from Stephens-Lee High School, she went to the Winston Salem Teachers College, which was the first all Black college to offer a degree in elementary education. She taught at some of the schools in Asheville, including the first nursery school to open there. And she taught for many years at the Long Ridge/Anderson School in Mars Hill.

"I remember those kids out there playing … Days gone and forgotten. The history and memories from that school mean so much.

"If I needed anything for my kids (students), I would just go down to Marshall to the Superintendent's office and tell them, and they would get it for us. And Mrs. Van over at Mars Hill College would always make sure we had everything we needed; she would see to it."

"Everybody was happy, there were no conflicts; parents were very understanding."

"I used to have a school choir. I played the piano and the children sang. In the mornings we would do devotions and then sing. On the warm days, we would have the windows open, and people would be standing outside listening to those little children pray and then sing. Sometimes we would go to Mt. Olive church and sing."

"We had coal heat in the school, and there's not one time that the school was cold. It was always warm."

"Sometimes it was hazardous getting there. If it rained, the road would be all slick and we'd slide. Little children would be covered in mud by the time they got to the school. Someone would always come to your rescue. It could be hazardous but it was always a joy. God provided a lot for us."

Wilson is married to Levie Wilson, who recently celebrated his 101st birthday. They now live in Asheville, but they maintain ties to the Mt. Olive Baptist Church in Mars Hill.

Mary Wilson taught for many years at the Long Ridge/Anderson School in Mars Hill.

"Everybody was happy, there were no conflicts; parents were very understanding."

Reprinted with permission of MHU and author.

Our Story, This Place

Charity Ray Remembers Student Life

by Loretta Atkins, from the Hilltop, the student newspaper of Mars Hill College, 2008

Charity Ray, curriculum library coordinator at Mars Hill College, went to school at Long Ridge.

At the time there were about 40 students with two teachers. "The building was divided into two rooms by a sliding door. One teacher would teach first through fourth grades, while the second teacher would teach grades five through eight, only being separated by that sliding door."

The textbooks that they had were torn and battered. "Our text books were actually donated. When the White schools got their new books, they would donate their old ones to the Colored schools."

Ray says commencement and May Day were two of the activities she remembers most about Long Ridge. "Commencement time was nice. Everything was held outside. A platform and stage would be built, and our parents were always invited to come. We always did the May Pole. We would have all those different colors and would just go around and around, weaving them, until the whole pole was covered."

The students at Long Ridge had to bring their lunches every day. There was no lunchroom or kitchen. There wasn't even an indoor bathroom or running water.

Across from the school where the cemetery now is stands a flagpole. This area was once a place of laughter and energy, for it was once a playground for the students. "We used to go down in the woods beside the schoolhouse and swing on grape vines. There was a little path we would take to get water from the stream, and there were grapevines down there so we would swing on them.

"Our school day would start around 8 a.m. and we'd leave around 2 p.m. because the kids had to get home. Some of the kids lived in Marshall, and some lived as far away as Hot Springs." Basic subjects were taught at Long Ridge, reading, writing and arithmetic, along with crafts. "We would get clay out of the banks and make things like clay pots and so forth."

Ray said one of the most significant things about Long Ridge was: "Even though there were hardships, we were determined to have an education."

> "The building was divided into two rooms by a sliding door. One teacher would teach first through fourth grades, while the second teacher would teach grades five through eight, only being separated by that sliding door."

Reprinted with permission of MHU and author.

The Historic Mars Hill Anderson Rosenwald School

Reflecting on Changes

by Teresa Buckner, Spring 2009 issue of From These Stones, *a Mars Hill College magazine*

Where the pavement ends on Mt. Olive Road in Mars Hill, there stands a remnant of a bygone era.

Peeking out from numerous too-close sapling trees and a few stray vines, the remains of the Long Ridge School are not that different from numerous other simple, boxy schoolhouses that once dotted the hills of Appalachia.

But the Long Ridge School is not like many other community-built one- and two-room schoolhouses throughout the region. The Long Ridge School was one of nearly 5,000 schools for Black children throughout the rural South built by the Rosenwald Initiative, a program funded by Julius Rosenwald, one-time president of Sears, Roebuck and Company.

"Oh, I can't even count how many of us there were that went to school there," Charity Ray said recently. "See, we had students that came up from Hot Springs and Marshall too."

At 72, Charity Ray has been a resident of Mars Hill for most of her life, and she has been an employee of Mars Hill College for 38 years. She began as a secretarial assistant in the president's office in 1970, but soon afterward, found her niche in the school's library.

These days, Charity works at a school that enjoys the largest student minority population of any college in western North Carolina. In her role as a library assistant, she sees and works with young people every day who have never known the sting of institutionalized segregation. Those young people have grown up in an America where their choices of friends, roommates, and even dates, are increasingly colorblind.

Many of them helped to elect America's first African American president, Barack Obama. When President Obama was sworn into office on January 20th, 2009, most of those students, whatever their racial or political background, realized that the event was a historic one. But it may be hard for them to honestly fathom how far America has come until they view see the story of segregation through the eyes of someone they know—like Charity.

"It seems almost like it never happened," she says. Matter-of-factly and without rancor, she tells about a time when there were places she could not go and things she could not do. And then, with characteristic optimism, she shakes her head and says, "You just cannot dwell on the hard times."

Like the Rosenwald school, Charity's memories tell a story of a time and a place when Americans were segregated at work, in their communities, at school, by the color of their skin.

"I had White friends that I played with and they didn't understand why we couldn't go to school together," Charity said. "But their parents explained it to them."

Charity's mother was an elementary student when Long Ridge Elementary was built. The school was funded by the Rosenwald Initiative, with additional funds from a local fundraising venture. According to Charity, local parents in the community made clay pots from the clay found near the school and sold the pots to make money toward the school's construction.

By the time Charity was in school, the Long Ridge School and Mt. Olive Church had become the center of life in Mars Hill's Black community. "All the Black people in Mars Hill bought land up around Mt. Olive so we could be near the school and the church," she said. Charity's mother did domestic work and her father sharecropped and did farm labor jobs on the side.

Charity Ray was a fifth-generation resident of the greater Mars Hill area. Her family first lived in a log cabin near the present Ingles grocery store, then built homes in the Long Ridge community. She was the daughter of John and Augusta Briscoe Ray, and sister to Christine Ray Rucker and Dorothy Ray Coone, both deceased.

Reprinted with permission of MHU and author.

Our Story, This Place

"I started school when I was five years old because my mother couldn't get a babysitter and the teacher said, 'Oh that's all right, just let her come on to school and I'll give her something to do,'" Charity said. "So that's how that happened."

What Charity did, mostly, in her words, was "doodle." The teacher gave her crayons and she drew picture after picture. It wasn't long before the teacher realized that Charity had a gift for art, and when Easter rolled around, she enlisted her youngest student to draw bunnies to decorate the blackboard.

"It was a gift; it wasn't anything I learned," she said. "I could always just look at something and then draw it." In the years since she discovered that gift, Charity has taken art classes and honed her artistic talent on canvas. She now sells her paintings in various local venues.

Charity attended the Long Ridge School through the eighth grade. At that point, she joined other African American students from Madison and Yancey counties in riding a public bus to Asheville. "The county paid for our tuition to go to a private school in Asheville because they didn't want integration," she said.

So she caught the bus on Main Street in Mars Hill and rode to Lexington Avenue in Asheville. She and her sisters then walked about a mile to Allen High School, a private school for Black girls near the present-day tunnel on Tunnel Road. At the end of each school day, Charity remembers lugging a heavy load of books back to the bus stop. She and the other Black students had to sit, or stand, in the back of the bus, even if there were seats available in the front.

"It did make you mad sometimes, because you were tired and you'd get to the bus and maybe you'd have to stand even if there were empty seats," she said. "You got angry and then that was it, because you didn't dare be rude. My parents wouldn't have stood for that."

The forced separation of White and Black children at the bus stop, on the bus and in school created fear and distrust. "I remember one time, some of the White kids thought that we had tails," she said, laughing. "But we told things on them too. It was just something that kids do," she said.

After graduation, Charity did domestic work for Dr. Hoyt Blackwell, the president of Mars Hill College. But she knew that she didn't want that life forever. "I was determined not to be domestic for the rest of my life," she said. So, during a visit to a cousin in New York City, she decided to stay.

Charity worked at a department store in New York for about ten years. It was during this time that she heard about a Baptist preacher from Memphis who was making waves for his moving sermons about racial equality. Not one to be an activist, she never went to hear Martin Luther King, Jr. speak, even when he was in New York City, but she was impressed with his words.

"I felt like it was going to take time for there to be equality, but I thought the direction he was taking was in line with what Christians would think, that you don't return evil for evil," she said. A woman of deep faith, Charity applies scripture to every area of her life. "You should be bold in your beliefs, especially if they are according to scripture, but violence just never solved anything."

Sometime later, Charity had "a feeling" that she should return home for a visit.

While in Mars Hill, her father was diagnosed with pancreatic cancer. Soon after his death, Charity's mother got cancer and eventually passed away as well. Charity stayed with her parents through their illnesses, while months turned into years. She never returned to her job in New York.

Charity passed away in 2020. She spent her later years working to rehabilitate the Mars Hill Anderson Rosenwald School, where she began her work as an artist at age five.

The original Mt. Olive Church, painting by Charity Ray.

Reprinted with permission of MHU and author.

The Historic Mars Hill Anderson Rosenwald School

"I started school when I was five years old because my mother couldn't get a babysitter and the teacher said, 'Oh that's all right, just let her come on to school and I'll give her something to do.'"

Reprinted with permission of MHU and author.

Not long after returning to Mars Hill, Charity became the pianist for Mt. Olive Church, a position she held for over 30 years. And in 1970 she took a secretarial position at Mars Hill College. Charity and a few other people from Mt. Olive Church formed a small singing group, and for several years, they traveled to various churches in Madison County to sing. "In that way, we made so many friends in Madison County," she said.

Among the group of singers who traveled from church to church was Charity's uncle, Manuel Briscoe, a well-known employee of the town of Mars Hill for many years. Briscoe had a reputation among older folks in Mars Hill as a godly man of character, and in fact, a small monument on Main Street commemorates his many contributions to the town.

It has been thus, in small and seemingly inconsequential ways, that Charity and her church family have fought—without fighting—a cultural racism that relegated them to a segregated school as small children.

"The color of your skin is just pigment," she tells students at Mars Hill College when professors invite her to address a class. "All blood runs red."

Charity's brand of "activism" is gentle and loving, and recognizes that even the right words do not always make for equality. "Hatred and prejudice are things that happen in your heart, and it takes a heart change. You can act one way, but you can feel another way," she said.

Not long ago, she was asked if she thought that she and the other Mt. Olive singers had had a positive impact on race relations in Madison County through the years. "I think maybe we did," she says, smiling. "Maybe we did."

The Long Ridge School, painting by Charity Ray.

Sisters Dorothy Coone and Charity Ray stand in front of the school in 2012.

> **The Rosenwald school building program had a widespread impact on black education in the South, and its effects were felt for decades.**

Endnotes for Memories and Stories

The Water Story on Long Ridge, p. 36

1. Pauline Cheek, "Briscoe Retires After 34 Years in Mars Hill," *The Asheville Citizen*, June 6, 1984, p. 13.
2. Madison County Board of Education Minutes, March 6, 1939.
3. Ibid., Sept. 6, 1943.
4. Oralene Simmons and Charity Ray Memories, 2014.

Black Folkways in Madison County: Doctors, p. 36

5. *The History of Blacks in Madison County: 1860-1981; Mars Hill College Scholar's Research*, 1981; Mars Hill University Archives, Local History, Box 1, p. 13.

Viola Barnette, Crusader for Black Education, p. 42

1. Wilson, Emily, *Hope and Dignity: Older Black Women of the South, Afro-American Women—North Carolina*, Philadelphia, PA: Temple University Press, 1983, pp 172-173.
2. Elizabeth D. Squire, "Viola Barnette, a Pioneer in Black Education," *The News Record*, May 25, 1983, p. 4.; *Madison County Heritage Book*, Vol. 1, p. 10.

Black Politics in Madison County, pg 42

1. "The History of Blacks in Madison County: 1860–1981," *Mars Hill College Scholar's Research*, 1981. Mars Hill University Archives, Local History, Box 1, p. 17.

Flora "Flo" Young Barnette, p. 44

1. Young, Perry Deane, *Our Young Family*, p. 475, 2003.
2. Wilson, Emily, *Hope and Dignity: Older Black Women of the South*, pp. 172-173, 1983.
3. Akins, Loretta, *Charity Ray Remembers Student Life*, MHU Hilltop Online, 2008.
4. Flora Barnette Interview by Richard Dillingham, March 23, 2022.

Memories of Family, Community, and School, pp. 45-47

1. 1940 Madison County, North Carolina Census, Transcribed by Lisa Bass and Shirley Crowder, pp. 409-411, 2013.
2. Harley Jolley, *The CCC of North Carolina, 1933-1942*, p. 79, 2007.
3. Mrs. Hart is preparing the Family History with pictures for Posterity.
4. Interview, Sarah Roland Weston Hart, April 1, 2022, at son Oscar Weston's home on Long Ridge by Richard Dillingham.
5. David Gilbert, "Unveiling Our Treasures," MHU Ramsey Center, 2020.

Integration

> On April 6, 1964, "Mr. Day, Colored Attorney at Law from Asheville, and Mr. Roland, Colored Jeweler from Asheville, met with the Board of Education concerning the integration of our schools."
>
> Chairman Manuel Briscoe, brother to Augusta Briscoe Ray, mother of Charity and Dorothy Ray, and Arseamous Roland, father of Sarah Hart, worked with the Madison County Board of Education, making the integration of schools a peaceful process.

Integration

Madison County, North Carolina Board of Education Minutes Related to the Mars Hill Colored School[1]

1963 - Sep. 2: "Chairman Ponder called the meeting to order at which time Geraldine Griffin, Colored lady from the Mars Hill Colored School, appeared before the Board to assign her child, who is in the fourth grade in the Mars Hill Colored School, to the Asheville School Unit. After discussing the pros and cons with Mrs. Griffin, it was decided to let her child remain in school at Mars Hill on a two weeks trial to make the necessary adjustments, at which time the Superintendent will check frequently with Mrs. Brown, teacher of the Mars Hill Colored School, to see if he could make suggestions for these adjustments." Later... "Motion made by Mr. Reese, seconded by Mr. Gardner, that Mr. Seam Roland, Janitor of the Mars Hill Colored School, salary be increased to $35.00 per month. This motion carried."

1964 - Apr. 6: 10:00 A.M. at Superintendent's office. "Mr. Day, Colored Attorney at Law from Asheville, and Mr. Roland, Colored Jeweler from Asheville, met with the Board of Education concerning the integration of our schools. After a lengthy discussion, Mr. Day said that he represented the N.W.A.C.P. [sic] and the cases in which he had taken to court, he had not lost. At 3:30 P.M. the school committee from the Mars Hill Colored School, along with Mrs. Geraldine Griffin, came to Marshall concerning integration. The number of persons at this hearing were taken to the courtroom at which time the discussion was intervened. Mr. Manuel Briscoe, Chairman of the Colored School Committee, made a triple barrel recommendation: (1) To build a new building for the Colored students; (2) To give them an additional teacher; (3) Place Mrs. Geraldine Griffin's child in the Mars Hill School Unit, of which she made the request. After discussing this, the Board of Education came to the following conclusion: For them to go back, have another meeting, and meet with the Board of Education the first Monday in June and come with a reasonable request."

1964 - Jun. 1: "The Colored School Committeemen of Mars Hill, along with Mr. Roland, a Colored Jeweler of Asheville, Mr. Jesse Ray of Asheville, Mr. Shields, of WMMH Radio, Mr. Story of the News-Record, Mr. Havlecheck of the Asheville-Citizen, and Mr. Leake, Madison County Attorney, met concerning the integration of the Mars Hill Colored and White Schools at Mars Hill. Chairman Ponder reviewed the last minutes that the Colored people met with the Board of Education. Mr. Briscoe verified this report and presented a written request of Mrs. Geraldine Griffin to assign her child to the Mars Hill White School. Mr. Briscoe asked that they might have a little more time and come back with other written requests concerning the Colored situation at Mars Hill. This request was granted. Chairman Ponder suggested that they meet back at 9:30 P.M."

1964 - Jun. 1: 9:30 P.M. "The Colored people from Mars Hill and Marshall at the request of the Chairman of the School Committee, Mr. Manuel Briscoe, and the Chairman of the Madison County Board of Education, Mr. Zeno H. Ponder, met with the Board of Education at 9:30 P.M. Present from Mars Hill were the following: Manuel Briscoe, Gudger Barnett, Seam Roland, Mrs. Augusta Ray, Mrs. Irene McDowell, Mr. Ervin; Present from Marshall were the following: Mrs. Presnell, Hugh Barnett, and three of the Presnell children; Present from Asheville were the following: Mr. Jesse Ray and Mr. Roland."

This meeting was held in the courtroom at which time Mr. Ponder, Chairman, explained the minutes of meetings in the past. Mr. Roland stated that Mr. Day, Attorney for the N.W.A.C.P. [sic], called and said he was in Atlanta, Georgia, and asked Mr. Roland and Mr. Ray to meet with the Colored people and the Madison County Board of Education. Mr. Roland and Mr. Ray would represent the N.W.A.C.P. [sic].

After several adjournments, the Board came up with the following conclusion after written requests were made for their children to be assigned at the Mars Hill White School: Jean Dobbins was assigned to the first grade at the Mars Hill White School, whose father is Gudger Barnett. Phillip M. Ervin was assigned to the 7th Grade at the Mars Hill White School, whose father is Ernest Ervin. Betty McDowell and Anne McDowell were assigned at the Mars Hill White School by the request of their mother, Mrs. Irene McDowell. Vicki Louise Wilson, daughter of Mrs. Geraldine Griffin, maid of Dr. Duck, who made a written request two months ago, was assigned to Grade 5 in the Mars Hill White School. All other requests were denied due to the inability among the parents to make an all out effort to integrate the Anderson School with the Mars Hill School. The meeting adjourned.

1965 - Apr. 27: [Principals and School Committeemen meet with Board of Education.] "The Civil Rights Program, better known as Title VI, was discussed. The following people were asked to make statements concerning the Civil Rights Program: Plato Reese made a statement for the integration program and stated that it had worked very successfully at the Mars Hill School. Fred Dickerson, Principal of Mars Hill School, concurred with Mr. Reese's statement. Mrs. John Ray (Colored) stated that the children were doing fine in the integrated situation at Mars Hill. Mr. A.E. Leake, Board Attorney, stated that we had no other course to follow except to follow the law and integrate the schools. Mr. Briscoe (Colored) stated that he didn't think that there would be any trouble in the integration."

"After the hearing of the school committeemen all over the county, the Board adjourned to the Judge's quarters and Chairman Ponder polled the voters of integration. Upon returning to the courtroom, motion made by Mr. Reese to integrate the schools of Madison County into their respective school districts for the 1965-66 school year. That the Anderson School will be closed at the end of this school year. This was seconded by Mr. Gardner, and passed unanimously."

Integration Memories[1]

"Integration of the schools went better than I thought it would go.

Declining the offer of help from an Asheville lawyer, Briscoe "felt on the spot" as a member of the school [committee], but he says, "I sought to maintain harmony. We had opposition on both sides, but it didn't get out of hand. We just worked together as people and didn't even lose friendship!"

~ *Chairman Manuel Briscoe*

The Historic Mars Hill Anderson Rosenwald School

Story of the School Building after Integration

During the last years of the 1900s, the building was used as a burley tobacco air-curing barn by the James Briscoe family.

After 1965, the Mars Hill Anderson Rosenwald School building remained the property of the Madison County Board of Education. In 2009, the Friends Group was organized to rehabilitate the building.

During the late 1960s, the building was used by the Buncombe-Madison Opportunity Corporation, which secured use of the building for a possible Long Ridge Youth Recreation Center. A young African American Asheville male was retained to develop the center. This idea for the use of the old school building for a recreation center was great for the youth, but not for the adults of the community. Therefore, the Recreation Center only operated for a few months. However, the basketball goals remained on each of the building end walls, where local Black and White youth gathered and played basketball. These youth left their team chalk marks and scores on the walls along with their initials, even some of them adding plus and love marks beside initials. Many of those youth are now our adult leaders, "and still great friends!"[1]

During the last years of the 1900s, the building was used as a burley tobacco air-curing barn by the James Briscoe family. Uncle James added small tree tier-poles in the building for hanging sticks of tobacco for curing. (He surely had leased the tobacco allotment of one of his White neighbors, as the tobacco acreage was regulated through the local Farm Office by the federal program.)

James was one of many children of Gilbert and Fannie Henson Briscoe. His sister Augusta Ray and brothers Dave Briscoe and Manuel Briscoe were also of the Long Ridge Community.[2]

For many years James worked as a painter for Jackie Shepherd, Shepherd's Enterprises. After completing a trailer paint job for Mr. Shepherd, to James' surprise, the newly painted trailer title was given to the Briscoes. With the help of his White friend L. C. Chandler, the mobile home was set up on Long Ridge, replacing their older trailer, where they lived out their lives. James was buried in the Mount Olive Cemetery, where the Mars Hill VFW Chapter erected a Flag Memorial for veterans of the community, James being a WWII Army veteran.[3]

In the early 2000s, a big tree fell on the building's addition, causing damage to the main building's roof. The Friends Group secured resources for a new building roof in 2011.[4]

Lasting Memories

High school students were bused to Stephens-Lee High School in Asheville after the 1940s, a practice that continued until Mars Hill schools were fully integrated by 1965.

The empty building continued standing after integration, being used as a recreation center and a basketball court by local youth, and later as a burley tobacco air-curing barn for the Briscoes in the 1980s.

The building continued to be owned by the Madison County School Board, but forgotten by Board Members until a local Long Ridge neighbor requested that the building be removed for widening the road by the school. Board of Education member Stewart Coates, who had grown up in the neighborhood, suggested that the historic building be given back to the Long Ridge Community for preservation. Thus the building was not torn down, but has survived for posterity.

See Stewart Coates letter on page 101

During interviews, Rosenwald alumni shared happy memories from their school years: fun games during recess; special events at Thanksgiving, Christmas, May Day, and graduation; walking to school, riding the bus, or going home for lunch.

Art, crafts, music, and dance were choice memories. Even a ruler or two on the palm of the hand was recalled with laughter.

The Historic Mars Hill Anderson Rosenwald School

Charity Ray Remembers the Long Ride to Education

by Nicole Robinson & Mee Vang, from the Hilltop, *student newspaper of Mars Hill College, 2008*

Charity Ray recalls being a young high school student, waiting at 7 o'clock in the morning for the public bus to take her from Mars Hill to Allen High School in Asheville.

This was in the early 1950s, during the time of Jim Crow Laws, when Black passengers were forced to sit in the back of the bus and to stand if there were not enough seats.

Often the bus was crowded, which meant that she would have to stand, holding her heavy textbooks, for the entire hour-long ride. "It wasn't the bus company's fault; it was the law at the time," said Ray.

She recalled an incident that happened on the bus one morning when the bus driver hit a pothole which caused her head to hit the top of the bus. "I had to go to the doctor. It really punctured the top of my head. It gave me a headache. So he stopped and got me some BC (aspirin). I will never forget that. Anyway, he was a nice person."

Ray looked at her experiences on the bus as an opportunity, not as a hardship. She would not have gone to high school at all if her friend and neighbor Viola Barnette had not lobbied for the buses that took Black children to school in Asheville. Black children were not allowed to attend the much closer all-White high school in Madison County. Ray spoke recently about Viola Barnette and about her own educational and personal experiences over the past fifty years.

"I enjoyed going to school. When you're younger you don't look at those things as problems," Ray said. The hardship was back at home doing chores.

When she reached Asheville, she walked to Allen High School. Allen was an all-girls, private, boarding school, but Charity did not board there. The school was an old house when she went to school there. The students were all Black, but there were both Black and White teachers. She graduated in 1955 with 30 classmates.

During that time period, Black students in Mars Hill went to Long Ridge School, which went up to eighth grade when Ray was a student there. It had only two classrooms in it and no indoor bathroom. Barnette and Ray's mother both wanted a bathroom to be put in the school or for a new school to be built. But they were told it would cost the county too much to build a new school.

Ray remembers Viola Barnette as very kind and always helping someone out. When Charity was growing up, her family was very close to Viola Barnette's family. Barnette helped the local Mount Olive Baptist Church, and she visited the sick. Ray recalls seeing Viola Barnette once a week at church. "I always went to the elderly people because I knew I was going to get wisdom from them," said Ray. She respected Viola Barnette most for her honesty.

The community was one where "everyone raised everyone else's children," said Ray. Mount Olive Baptist Church was the center. Ray and her family farmed. She recalls, "You didn't realize there was any kind of need because we always had plenty to eat."

Black children were not allowed to attend the much closer all-White high school in Madison County.

Reprinted with permission of MHU and author.

Our Story, This Place

Ray recalls a special time in her childhood when everybody met at the bottom of the hill by the river and washed clothes. "The younger people got the wood, and they had the iron pots that they built the fire under, and they boiled their clothes and used the lye soap, of course, that they had made themselves."

Ray works now as a Curriculum Librarian Coordinator in the Nash building at Mars Hill College. She continues to live in the Mars Hill community.

Black students in Mars Hill went to Long Ridge School, which went up to eighth grade when Ray was a student there. It had only two classrooms in it and no indoor bathroom.

When a 1954 Supreme Court ruling declared segregation in education unconstitutional, Rosenwald Schools became obsolete.

Endnotes for Integration

Madison County, North Carolina Board of Education Minutes Related to the Mars Hill Colored School, p. 56

1. *Madison County Board of Education Minutes, 1963–1965. Extracted by Pauline Cheek and Dan Slagle.*

Integration Memories, p. 57

1. *Interview by Pauline Cheek, "Briscoe Retires After 34 Years in Mars Hill," The Asheville Citizen, June 6, 1984, p. 13.*

Story of the School Building After Integration, p. 58

1. *Dr. Richard Hoffman Journals, 1960s, with comment by Jeanie Hoffman, 2019.*
2. *Nephew Dr. David Lloyd Briscoe information, 2019.*
3. *Jackie Shepherd, employer, and friend L.C. Chandler information, 2019.*
4. *MHARS Minutes, 2011.*

*Notable
Biographies*

Long Ridge Community Achievers

Five students from the Long Ridge community are given as examples of academic achievement and cultural contributions, from second to sixth school generations.

Kevin Barnette

Kevin Barnette

Kevin Barnette, grandson of Viola King Barnette, graduated from Mars Hill College in 1985, having been one of the school's star football players. He achieved his Masters Degree from the US Sports Academy at Daphne, Alabama. Kevin returned to his Alma Mater as Assistant Football Coach, where he works today. At Mars Hill University, he helped organize the Fellowship of Christian Athletes, one of the largest in the South. Further, Mr. Barnette is a member of the Madison County School Board. The Rev. Barnette serves as Associate Pastor at Brookstone Church at Flat Creek. He is a member of the Rosenwald Friends Group, serving as chair of the Community Relations Committee.

Dr. David Lloyd Briscoe

Dr. David Lloyd Briscoe

Dr. David Lloyd Briscoe grew up in the Long Ridge Community and attended the Long Ridge School. Also, he was a member of Boy Scout Troop 85 that met at the school, which he organized at age twelve. After receiving his PhD in Sociology from Southern Illinois University at Carbondale, he became a tenured professor of Sociology at the University of Arkansas at Little Rock.

He is a US Fulbright Scholar's Program Representative, a Graduate School Faculty Member, a Distinguished Teaching Fellow in the Department of Sociology and Anthropology, and coauthor of one book and author of four more. Today, he serves on the Boy Scouts of America National Executive Board, and is a recipient of the Silver Buffalo Award, the highest award in the Boy Scouts of America for distinguished service to youth on a national level. In the summer of 2019, he was a program presenter at the 24th World Scout Jamboree in West Virginia. He is the first Board of Advisors member with the Mars Hill Rosenwald School Friends' Group.

Charity Ray

Charity Ray working on a painting.

Charity Ray, retired from Mars Hill University School of Education and Library, was a local artist. Her water colors have been purchased by individuals from many states, and her renderings of the Mt. Olive Baptist Church building and the Mars Hill Rosenwald School building are published by the Friends Group. Her love for art began when she was allowed to sit in at the Long Ridge School at age five, where she began her first drawings. This was before the days of kindergarten. She continued her art work at Allen High School for African American girls in Asheville, where she graduated. She was a member of a Mars Hill arts group, The Church Mice. She was also a member of the History Committee of the Rosenwald Building Rehabilitation Project. Thanks go to the Rockefeller Room, her parents, and her teachers at Rosenwald Elementary and Allen High Schools, who encouraged her. Charity passed away on October 2, 2020.

Charlene Ray

Charlene Ray, great-great-great-granddaughter of Joseph Anderson, graduated from Mars Hill College in 1982 with honors. She was the first Appalachian Scholar at the school, receiving a full scholarship. For her senior research project, she researched and wrote, "History of Blacks in Madison County." After receiving her masters degree at Eastern Tennessee State University, she became a staff member at the Environmental Protection Agency in Washington, DC.

Charlene Ray

Sarah Roland Weston Hart

Mrs. Hart is a native of the Long Ridge Community in Mars Hill. She is the daughter of Arseamous (Seam) Roland and Mollie Carson Roland, who moved to the community in 1939, one of the first property owners on Long Ridge. She is one of eight siblings. The family moved from Yancey County to Long Ridge because of its school, church, and tobacco farming in Mars Hill. Her son, Oscar Weston still lives on the original Roland property.

After attending all eight grades at the Mars Hill Anderson Rosenwald School, she graduated from Stephens-Lee High School in Asheville. Sarah graduated from Mars Hill College in 1975, with a degree in Elementary Education, being the first African American to graduate from Madison County and her Long Ridge Community. She taught school in the Asheville City School System from 1975-1984.

After moving to Virginia, she taught school in Alexandra, VA, and in Prince William County. She received her Master's Degree in Organizational Leadership Management from George Mason University at Fairfax, Virginia. After retirement, Sarah returned home to NC in 2007.

Sarah is proud that her granddaughter, Stephanie Weston, continued the Roland family education tradition by graduating from Mars Hill University in 2007.

In April, 2020, Mission Hospital announced that Sarah Hart was awarded the Mission Hospital's Volunteer Service Award, "The Frist Volunteer Award."

Today, Sarah leads the Stephens-Lee Alumni Association; is a member with Zeta Phi Beta Sorority, the historically Black sorority that is a community-conscientious, action-oriented organization; volunteers at Christian Avery Learning Center, teaching and caring for children ages 2-16; and serves at the Mission/HCA Medication Assistant Program. Also, she volunteers with the Billy Graham Training Center at the Cove in Black Mountain, NC.

In 2020, Sarah was recognized and honored at the Liston B. Ramsey Center for Appalachian Studies by Mars Hill University at their "Unveiling our Treasures" by Dr. David Gilbert of the History Department.

Further, Mrs. Hart is serving as a member of the Mars Hill Anderson Rosenwald School's Friends Group and its History Committee for its publication of "Our Story, This Place."

Sarah Roland Weston Hart

Sarah Hart is the daughter of Arseamous (Seam) Roland and Mollie Carson Roland, who moved to the community in 1939. They were one of the first property owners on Long Ridge.

The Historic Mars Hill Anderson Rosenwald School

Oralene Anderson Graves Simmons

Oralene Anderson Graves Simmons, great-great-granddaughter of Joseph Anderson.

Oralene Anderson Graves Simmons attended the Long Ridge School in the Rosenwald building, and graduated from Stephens-Lee High School in Asheville, NC. She was the first African American admitted to Mars Hill College in 1961, one of the first admissions in the South, two years before Martin Luther King's famous speech, "I Have A Dream!" She is the great-great-granddaughter of Joseph Anderson. Her grandmother, Effie Anderson Coone, granddaughter of Joe Anderson, taught at the Mars Hill Colored School in 1901.

Oralene became a leader in Asheville during the integration protest years, later becoming Director of the YMI Cultural Center. She organized the Martin Luther King Prayer Breakfast in Asheville, the largest in the Southeast. Today, she continues her leadership in cultural diversity activities. She is a member of the Friends of the Mars Hill Rosenwald School Rehabilitation Project.

Members of Mars Hill University's student NAACP chapter spearheaded an effort to honor Ms. Simmons on Monday, October 12, 2015 by planting a weeping cherry tree. A plaque dedicated to Simmons was placed near the site of Joseph Anderson's memorial on Joe Anderson Drive.

Oralene Graves Simmons Historic Connections

The history of western North Carolina's slave economy became a stark reality for Oralene Graves when she enrolled at Mars Hill College in 1961. The first African American student admitted to the school, she had stronger and deeper ties to the institution than anyone else on campus. Her great-great-grandfather Joe Anderson was the slave who was held in jail as collateral for a debt to contractors who built the first building.

Oralene Graves Simmons is chair of Asheville's Martin Luther King Association.

"The Legacy," reproduced from the Rural Heritage Museum exhibit, 2014-15.

Article in Time *magazine, August 11, 1961*

The Historic Mars Hill Anderson Rosenwald School

Joe helped make bricks for the first Mars Hill College building, which was completed in 1856.

J.W. Anderson

After marriage, a family of five and grandchildren, and a long career with Asheville Parks and Recreation Department, following her studies at Mars Hill College, Oralene would retire and become chair of the Martin Luther King Association. While there, Oralene received a call from Hawaii, a complete stranger, who wanted to know if Oralene knew of someone named Jessie Woodson Anderson. The caller said that she was Susan Anderson, great-great-granddaughter of J. W. Anderson, owner of Oralene's enslaved ancestor Joseph Anderson.

In 1999, the Joseph Anderson family was recognized as one of the Founding Families of Mars Hill College.

Oralene (L) and cousin Susan Anderson.

(L-R) Roy, Susan, Oralene, and Scott at the Joe Anderson memorial.

Our Story, This Place

Mars Hill University Honors Oralene Simmons

Mars Hill University's spring 2022 commencement ceremony honored not only nearly 175 graduates, but also the university's first African American student.

Oralene Simmons, who broke the color barrier in the early 1960s, was presented an honorary doctorate. The commencement speaker was Preston Blakely, mayor of Fletcher, North Carolina, and Simmons's grandson. The commencement took place in Moore Auditorium on Saturday, May 21, 2022.

Oralene Anderson Graves Simmons is a Mars Hill native who has become a well known figure in the Asheville area for her decades of work in the community and in the Civil Rights arena. Among many other contributions, she founded the Martin Luther King Jr. Prayer Breakfast in Asheville; was executive director of the YMI Cultural Center; and served as the cultural arts supervisor for the City of Asheville. Oralene, who attended Mars Hill College from 1961-1963, was the first African American student to enroll at the institution.

Oralene attended the Long Ridge School in the Rosenwald building and graduated from Stephens-Lee High School in Asheville, NC. She was the first African American admitted to Mars Hill College in 1961, one of the first admissions in the South, two years before Martin Luther King's famous speech, "I Have A Dream!" She is the great-great-granddaughter of Joseph Anderson. Her grandmother, Effie Anderson Coone, granddaughter of Joe Anderson, taught at the Mars Hill Colored School in 1901.

Oralene became a leader in Asheville during the integration protest years, later becoming Director of the YMI Cultural Center. She organized the Martin Luther King Prayer Breakfast in Asheville, the largest in the Southeast. Today, she continues her leadership in cultural diversity activities. She is a member of the Friends of the Mars Hill Rosenwald School Rehabilitation Project.

Preston Blakely is in his first term as mayor of the Henderson County town of Fletcher. He grew up in Fletcher, graduated from Asheville High School, and received bachelor's degrees in political science and African American & African diaspora studies at UNC Greensboro and a master's in public affairs at Western Carolina University. He was elected to town council in 2019 and won last fall's mayoral election. At 27 years old, he is Fletcher's youngest mayor in its 33-year existence, and is its second African American mayor.

About Mars Hill University

Mars Hill University is a premier private, liberal arts institution offering over 30 baccalaureate degrees, as well as master's degrees in criminal justice, elementary education, teaching, and management. Founded in 1856 by Baptist families of the region, the campus is located just 20 minutes north of Asheville in the mountains of western North Carolina. Visit www.mhu.edu.

Oralene Simmons

Oralene's grandmother, Effie Anderson Coone, granddaughter of Joe Anderson, taught at the Mars Hill Colored School in 1901.

Preston Blakely, mayor of Fletcher, North Carolina

The Billy Strayhorn Connection

In March 1910 the mother and father of Billy Strayhorn, the eminent African American composer-arranger, were married in the Mars Hill African American church, Piney Grove Church. It was located on Walker Branch of Paint Fork and Little Ivy. The Strayhorn family remembered the wedding having taken at the church in "wooded Mars Hill." Both his mother, Lillian Young, and his maternal grandmother, Alice Young, must have attended the Colored schools in the Mars Hill area, as mother Lillian was well educated.

Lillian Young Strayhorn

The Strayhorn family: mother Lillian, James Jr., Billy, Lillian, Georgia, Theodore, and James. John, who took the photo, is kneeling in front.

Billy Strayhorn (1915–1967) was one of the greatest composers in the history of American music, the creator of a body of work that includes such standards as "Take the 'A' Train." Yet all his life Strayhorn was overshadowed by his friend and collaborator Duke Ellington, with whom he worked for three decades as the Ellington Orchestra's ace songwriter and arranger.[1]

These words come from the back jacket of David Haidu's biography of Billy Strayhorn.[2] In the book he writes about Billy's family and background in Mars Hill.

> Eighteen-year-old Lillian Young, the only child of Alice Young, a single mother from a comfortable working family in wooded Mars Hill, North Carolina, was attentively raised and well educated.
>
> She graduated from a two-year program for women at Shaw University, a Baptist school whose curriculum stressed ladylike manners and social skills. Poised and soft-spoken, with an eye for modest, womanly clothes and an ear for elegiac language ("I see the rain is slackening"), she earned a lifelong reputation for formality.
>
> Lillian and twenty-year-old James Nathaniel Strayhorn were married in a Baptist Church ceremony in wooded Mars Hill on March 10, 1910.
>
> James, a descendant of the founder of the first whiskey distillery established in the South after the Civil War, was also raised in relative comfort and style in a roomy Prairie Victorian house in the Black section of Hillsborough, North Carolina. A firecracker of a man, James seemed a perfect counterbalance to Lillian, as ebullient as she was sedate, as spontaneous as she was doctorial, as adventurous as she was restrained. They made an exquisite-looking couple: willowy, elegant Lillian, with her curly, pulled up hair, her clear, open eyes, and a soft smile that nudged two sets of double dimples on her cheeks; and thick-set towering James with his glistering liquid eyes and broad, sly, cocksure attitude.
>
> Their fourth child ,and third boy, was born in 1915 without a legal name on his birth certificate, just Baby Boy Strayhorn. At age five, he was given the name William Strayhorn, but everybody called him Billy.

His love of music began early with his mother and Grandmother Strayhorn at Hillsborough, when visiting there during his summers. By the time he reached high school, his classmates called him "Talent." Talent. Talent. That was Billy. "Everybody was in awe of Billy, you know, because of his music." "…he was just like, you'd say, a genius." His first jazz composition, "Lush Life," was composed while he was still in high school.

Billy Strayhorn's professional jazz career brought him international fame with Duke Ellington, Louis Armstrong, Lena Horne, and others.

David Hajdu, Author and Jazz Musician

David Hajdu, author of *Lush Life,* the biography of Jazz musician, Billy Strayhorn, came to Mars Hill in the 1990s, in search of information on Strayhorn's mother, Lillian Young and grandmother Alice Young.

He agreed to come to Cullowhee and speak to the student body at WCU during Black Heritage Celebrations, if someone would take him to Mars Hill for research on Billy Strayhorn's maternal family, the Youngs. WCU Professor Dr. Anderson called Richard Dillingham for help. They came to Long Ridge, interviewing Charity Ray and Dorothy Coone and visiting the Mount Olive Cemetery, looking for the Young graves, but the mother's and grandmother's graves are not there.

Dillingham had made arrangements for them to visit the Gardner property, located on Walker Branch of Paint Fork of Little Ivy in Madison County, NC, where the Black Piney Grove Church stood, and the Strayhorn parents were married in the church in 1910, beside the Black graveyard. Dr. Anderson parked the car in the drive to a single-wide farm renter's mobile home. As Mr. Haidju was allergic to poison oak, Dr. Anderson and Dillingham climbed the hill, leaving the visiting author in the car.

While on the hill, looking for Young graves, a redneck came out from the mobile home and asked, "Why are you here?" Mr. Hajdu informed the young man that we were looking for graves of the Black Youngs. Do you know anything about the Black graveyard on the hill?." He responded, "Yes, you see that big White Oak up there? We hung those N---------- in that tree and buried them right there, under the tree!" The encounter was related by Mr. Hajdu.

No Young graves were found, and the Southern Appalachian White men departed with Mr. Hajdu, being embarrassed by our bigoted neighbor.[1]

David Hajdu's *Lush Life* was published in 1996, and received the ASCAP Deems Taylor Award for *Lush Life* in 1997. Further, the *New York Times* editors picked *Lush Life* for its list of 100 best books of all time.

Mr. Hajdu, a prolific author and jazz musician, is music critic for *The Nation* and professor at the Columbia University School of Journalism.[2]

Duke Ellington & Billy Strayhorn

Billy Strayhorn's professional jazz career brought him international fame with Duke Ellington, Louis Armstrong, Lena Horne, and others.

David Hajdu

The Historic Mars Hill Anderson Rosenwald School

David L. Briscoe, the Boy Scout

Dr. David Lloyd Briscoe

When Black children completed the sixth grade at Anderson Elementary School they were bused to Hill Street Junior High School, Lucy Herring Junior High, or Stephens-Lee High School in Asheville.

I recall very vividly going to the Christmas parades for several years at the town of Mars Hill in the early 1960s. As a young lad, I was so thrilled to see all the beautiful floats, marching bands, and crowds of people who seemed to be just as excited as I was.

I noticed that in the parade, there were many young boys dressed in khaki uniforms. I was so impressed to watch them march as if they were young soldiers. I did not know they were Boy Scouts. As a matter of fact, I had never heard of the Boy Scouts. After attending several Christmas parades, I found out that these young boys were Boy Scouts, and oh, how I wanted to be one of them. These boys were from Troop 102 in Mars Hill. This troop was an all-White troop, and I knew I could not join that troop because of segregation.

When Black children completed the sixth grade at Anderson Elementary School, located in the Black community on Long Ridge Road, they were bused to Hill Street Junior High School, Lucy Herring Junior High, or Stephens-Lee High School in Asheville, North Carolina if the student was in high school.

When I was in the seventh grade at Lucy Herring Elementary School, once a week our class would go to the library. I noticed in the magazine rack a copy of *Boy's Life* magazine. Little did I know that this monthly publication was published by the Boy Scouts of America. After reading the magazine, I became even more interested in the Boy Scouts.

At Hill Street Junior High School, I met a young Black youth who was a scout in one of the Black troops in Asheville. He had a battered Boy Scout handbook. He showed it to me and I later offered to purchase it from him. He sold it to me for $1. I fell in love with every aspect of the book. By the way, I still have that handbook after all these years in my library at home. I have often looked through the handbook from time to time and have enjoyed the memories of yesteryear.

There was a statement in the book that said if you lived too far out in the country where a troop did not exist, just send a letter to the national office and request some assistance. I did that very thing, I wrote to the national office requesting assistance, and within a few weeks, I received a letter from the national office informing me that I lived in the jurisdiction of the Daniel Boone Council in Asheville, North Carolina. Within weeks, Frank Gay, the District Executive who worked for the local Boy Scout council met with my uncle, Mr. Manuel Briscoe.

My uncle was a respected community leader in both the Black and White communities, and he was the ideal person to lead Troop 85 as its scoutmaster, beginning June 30th, 1965. We had at least five or six boys in the troop. For a short time, we met at Anderson Elementary School, and we later held scout meetings at Mt. Olive Baptist Church on Long Ridge Road.

The names of some of the boys including myself were: Thomas Briscoe, Lawrence Briscoe, Michael Ervin, Junior Dobbs, David Wilson, and Harlen Wilson. Mr. Charles Wilson was listed as an Assistant Scoutmaster. My dad, Mr. David Briscoe, Mr. Ernest Ervin, and Mr. Bobby Briscoe were also listed as adult leaders. I will never forget when Mr. Bobby Hernandez, Scoutmaster of Troop 102 in Mars Hill visited a parents meeting held at the Anderson Elementary School to help our troop get started.

Over the years, our troop did a lot of hiking and camping in the Mars Hill area under the leadership of our Senior Patrol Leader and Patrol Leader. I attended summer camp with Troop 102 in 1967 and 1968. I returned to Camp Daniel Boone in the summer of 1968 to attend an aquatic camp to complete my lifesaving merit badge. This was one of the few merit badges I lacked in completing my requirements for Eagle.

I did complete all the requirements for the rank of Eagle Scout, and a board of review was scheduled for September 24th, 1968. I will never forget that my Eagle Scout Board of Review was held at Mars Hill Baptist Church. The members of my Board of Review were Mr. Alfred Huff, Mr. Joe Huff, Mr. Bobby Hernandez, and Mr. Max Hughes from Spruce Pine, North Carolina. Normally, board of reviews last for an hour or less, but not mine. My review lasted from 7:00 p.m. to 10:00 p.m. They reviewed me in detail on each of the twenty-one merit badges required for Eagle. I guess that was the reason my review lasted so long. Nevertheless, I passed the review and became an Eagle Scout! I became the first Black Eagle Scout in Mars Hill, and Madison County. Also, a relative, Kenneth Lofton became one of the first Black Eagle Scouts in the Daniel Boone Council in 1956.

I have remained active and registered in the Boy Scouts of America since joining the movement in 1965. I have served as Council President of the Quapaw Area Council in Arkansas, and a former member of the Boy Scouts of America National Executive Board, and the National Advisory Council. I have served on the BSA Southern Region Executive Board, and the BSA Southern Region Advisory Council. I have served on the staff of sixteen National and World Scout Jamborees. I am a recipient of Scouting's highest honors including the Distinguished Eagle Scout Award, the Silver Beaver Award, the Silver Antelope Award, the Silver Buffalo Award, the National Learning for Life Distinguished Service Award, and the National Elbert K. Fretwell Outstanding Educator Award.

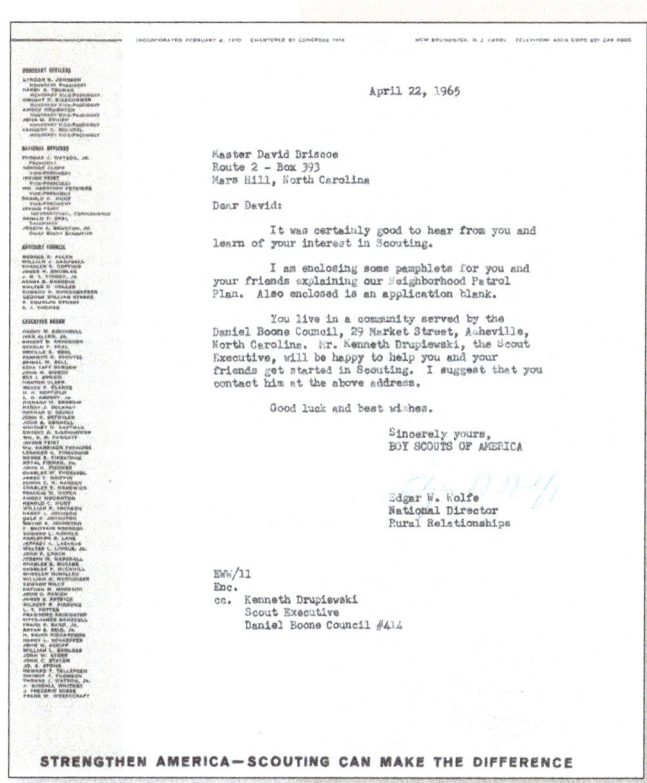

Letter sent to David from the national office of the Boy Scouts.

Manuel Briscoe, a respected community leader in both the Black and White communities, was the ideal person to lead Troop 85 as its scoutmaster at its founding in June 1965.

The Historic Mars Hill Anderson Rosenwald School

Omar Lewis McClain: The Journey

Omar McClain

The McClain family settled in Marshall, NC in the late 1800s.

This is a history of a place, the place, my place, where I began…

During the Civil War, the Union soldiers holed up in the first hotel in Hot Springs, NC. It became their headquarters. The hotel was called Warm Springs Hotel.[1] In 1862, Union sympathizers and the Confederate deserters raided the town of Marshall to get salt for winter,[2] and this event led to the Shelton Laurel Massacre in 1863.[3]

From the late 1800s until 1947, the Colored children of the laborers attended a county school for Colored students in Hot Springs, while the school children in Marshall attended classes sporadically, in the Ponders Baptist Church building on Hayes Run until around 1930.

The Warm Springs Hotel was shot-up badly, damaged beyond repair and it burned in 1863. It was replaced by the Mountain Park Hotel, which also burned in 1884[4], being replaced by a new building the next year. In the footprint of the two burned-out hotels, a third hotel was built predominantly by crews of Colored laborers from Tennessee. The last hotel fire took place in 1920 and the hotel was never rebuilt.[5]

By 1947, the children of Hot Springs had to catch a train from Hot Springs to Marshall, NC and then board a school bus with the children of Marshall for a ride to the Long Ridge School in Mars Hill.

Life began for me in the small town of Marshall, which was established 1851 and is the county seat of Madison County, NC, located on the banks of the French Broad River. My McClain family settled in Marshall in the late 1800s. By 1900, the Federal Census for that year, shows Marshall's population was 337 of which 1% were Colored people.[6]

My daddy, Omer McClain (or lovingly known as Boyd McClain), had the first and only Colored-owned-and-operated business in Marshall. In 1940, Omer and his wife Dora are listed with son Leonard, age 2. At age 24, Mr. McClain is listed as a valid business, as he purchased a building, originally the Machinist Garage.[7] Today, I can say my dad was an exceptional mechanic and businessman. Those in the community of Marshall knew and respected him and his quality of service. I remember, there were times when my mom and I would be working with him, watching him make his own tools for a particular job. We saw him as a genius mechanic.

When we relocated to Asheville in the summer of 1955, he continued his business which was located at the lower end of Coxe Ave. My older brother, Leonard, attended the Long Ridge School through to the 8th grade. Knowing that soon he would be leaving to attend Stephens-Lee High School in Asheville, and during his last year at the Long Ridge School, our mom, Lady Dora, said to Len, "Show your brother how to be prepared to be bused to the Long Ridge School." I was only 4 years old. He shared the details with me, held my hand of sorts, and prepared me for that early morning trek to school.

I had the opportunity to attend school through the fourth grade at the Long Ridge School; how exciting! My brother, however, faced his own challenges, catching the Greyhound bus in Marshall to go to high school in Asheville.[8]

As a student at Mars Hill Anderson Rosenwald School, I was an anxious child. Learning was very easy for me, but my high energy got me in trouble with my teacher, my aunt Mrs. Wilson, many, many times. Mathematics was my favorite class, but all learning was fun. Fellow students were like family, and most of them were.

After moving to Asheville, I attended Hill Street School, then the locally renowned Stephens-Lee High School. While in high school, I discovered my love for music, playing trombone in the Stephens-Lee High School band. During my tenure in high school, there would be annual workshops and events offered to high school bands, either in Raleigh or Durham, NC. The year I attended, a seminar was offered by Doc Severinson, band director of Johnny Carson's *Tonight Show* at the time. A profound training I will never forget, and am always grateful for, as it served me well in later years.

After graduating from high school, I enlisted in the US Army and became a member of the 82nd Airborne Division. With my musical experiences in high school and special training, the opportunity to play in the US Army Band evolved for me, to the point of playing in the USO Band, performing for the troops with such notables as Bob Hope, Stiller & Meara, and Joey Heatherton.

After my tour of duty, I relocated to New York City where my mom was living. Once I was settled in, I enrolled at Queens College and majored in Sociology. Eventually I found my way to Wall Street working in finance. After approximately 50-odd years in and around New York, I returned home to Asheville, NC to relax, live, and work.

Eventually, through the introduction of a dear friend, I became a member of the Mars Hill Anderson Rosenwald School Friends Group, making a full circle to the place where my education began, helping to rehabilitate my childhood schoolhouse, and returning to the Long Ridge community of Mars Hill, in Madison County, NC. What a great honor.

Omar played in the USO Band, performing for the troops with such notables as Bob Hope, Stiller & Meara, and Joey Heatherton.

Fatimah´ Shabazz: Walking My Walk… My Way

Fatimah´ Shabazz

Fatimah´ Shabazz, (a.k.a. Beverly Wilson) is the daughter of Mary H. Wilson, a teacher at the Mars Hill Anderson Rosenwald for fourteen years, 1939–1953.

As a small child, I can remember hearing my mom responding when I would say something like "I am going to run away," she would say "OK, but before you do, get a good education first." Just hearing these words slowed my process down to 'pay attention to her words' and in all actuality, it made sense and I trusted her, cause she was my schoolteacher and my mom.

The older I got, the less I thought about 'running away'; I did as she said and many, many years later her words would benefit me, even to this day, one thing I did know, education was the key for the best results in life … 'cause my mama said so. Even so, in the back of my mind, not to run away, but seek sustainable ways to escape Asheville, NC and my very strong-discipline mama.

My first school was the Mars Hill Anderson Rosenwald School, Mars Hill, NC, where my mom was a teacher. Each morning the process was: wake up very early, get dressed, eat breakfast, and mom would drive me across town to my grandma's house, and then drive to Mars Hill to teach. After a while this process got old and mom started taking me with her. I was able to be in the school at a very early age—3-½ years old. When I turned 4, mom enrolled me in school and I became a student.

When mom retired from Mars Hill Anderson Rosenwald School, she enrolled me in the Asheville City Schools System. For some unknown reason, the City School System felt that children educated in county schools where less educated than city school students, I should have gone into the 4th grade at Livingston Street; instead, I was put back one year. I remember feeling very, very disappointed and felt that mom should have challenged the B of E. It all worked out in any case. Attending Livingston Street School, I would walk up the street to my grandmother's house and wait for mom to get off work.

After Livingston Street School, I attended Hill Street School, which was just down the hill from our home, for six years, and where I joined the Hill Street Band. Then I moved on to Stephens-Lee High School, where I played saxophone in the renowned Stephens-Lee High School Band. After graduating, keeping those words from mom in mind about education, I choose to enroll in Blanton's Business College for one school term. My thinking at that time, was that business courses would be great, it could be my key to support my strong desire to depart Asheville and also good for a career.

The business course did not become a dedicated career, however, but knowledge of it supported other visions, goals, and aspirations I had. All along, I kept in mind ways to leave Asheville.

With a job as secretary at Hill Street Baptist Church—the business classes helped secure the job, in addition to the family connections I had (mom was church organist and dad was a Trustee)—I got married, moved away to Norfolk, VA, and at the tender age of 19-½, I landed in the State of California.

Once in California, it was and has been since a constant awakening and questioning—what, when, how, who etc. These are the questions I asked myself. OK, you are here, you made it all the way to California, what are you going to do? First thought that came to mind, go to school, get a job, and keep moving forward.

I enrolled in College of Alameda, for two years of study and received a degree in Marketing, Advertising and Merchandising with a focus in the fashion and entertainment industries. Attending college was a very high note for me. I was stimulated extensively by learning the skills of couture fashion designs and designing my own wardrobe, a fascinating time for me.

After completing college and graduating I continued to gain additional knowledge in San Francisco at California School of Fashion & Design. All the time I attended College of Alameda, and California School of Fashion & Design, I worked at House of Fabrics near Telegraph Ave. in Oakland, California.

In 1987 I returned home, worked at Ivey's Asheville Mall for exactly one year. Realizing home was not resonating with me quite yet, I returned to California, landing in Los Angeles this time. I acquired a fantastic job in Beverly Hills on Beverly Blvd. Here I had the opportunity to meet Hollywood's costume designers for renowned actors, actresses, music artists, and more. Eventually, my opportunities expanded, and I was able to work within my passion, the fashion industry and one of my loves, music and the entertainment industries.

Some years later, returning home, once again, and once again I was not ready, or the time or Asheville was not quite ready for me. I moved to Atlanta, worked at a fine arts gallery in Stone Mountain, Ga. In addition to being cured of big city energies living in Atlanta, I also received a notice, it was time for me to be home and take care of my parents. I returned home in 1993 right before that famous big blizzard, amd have been here ever since.

Afterwards my focus became caring for my mom and dad, Levie and Mary Wilson. A constant combination of challenging yet blessed times, loving and learning about them both, and about the town and people I grew-up in and with. Old stuff, yet a whole lot of new.

I was deeply honored, and continue to be, for the opportunity to care for mom until she passed in 2009 at the young age of 96, and for my papa's passing in 2013 at the young age of 107.

Currently, I am a potent participant as an alumna, as the Chair for the Alumni Committee of Mars Hill Anderson Rosenwald School, co-creator of the Mars Hill Anderson Rosenwald School newsletter, and dedicated to accessing descendants of alumni of the Mars Hill Anderson Rosenwald School.

Fatimah´ currently lives in Asheville and serves as leader of the Friends Alumni Group. She is also a professional musician, percussionist, and vocalist, and the owner, CEO, and host of the internet TV channel, WRNU.

Rev. Dr. William E. Ray, Sr.

William, son of Roy and Pauline Ray, was born on June 27, 1950 in Mars Hill, NC. He married Brenda L. Ray, May 14, 1989 and they have four children and nine grandchildren.

Education

- Attended grades 1-5 at Anderson Elementary School, Mars Hill, NC
- Moved to Asheville when he was 13 years old and attended Asheville City Schools
- Graduated from Asheville High School in 1970
- Earned Doctor of Divinity from Shaw University, Raleigh, NC
- ThD/PhD Degree Omni Bible University, Forest City, Pastoral Ministry/Biblical Studies
- Certified Christian Counselor
- Certified Bishop Full Gospel Fellowship of America

Work Experience

- Pastor, Welfare Baptist Church Asheville, NC for 17 years
- Retired from Mars Hill University, 2010

Nationally Known Rosenwald School Alumni[1]

Author **Maya Angelou** graduated from the Lafayette County Training School, a Rosenwald School in Stamps, Arkansas. She wrote about her experiences at the school in her most famous work, *I Know Why the Caged Bird Sings* in 1969. She received over fifty honorary degrees.

US Representative **John Lewis** attended a Rosenwald School in Pike County, Alabama. He was elected to the US House of Representatives. He was awarded the Presidential Medal of Freedom.

Pulitzer Prize-winning journalist **Eugene Robinson** attended the Felton Training School, a Rosenwald School located near Orangeburg, South Carolina. He received the Pulitzer Prize in 2009.

Acclaimed American playwright and director **George C. Wolf** attended the Rosenwald Laboratory School in Frankfort, Kentucky. Wolf won a Tony Award in 1993 as director of *Angels in America: Millennium Approaches*.

During the groundbreaking in November 2015.
Left to right: Earl Conley, Sarah Roland Weston Hart, Eugene Jones, Charity Ray, Omar McClain, Fatimah´ Shabazz, Gladys Koon Gibson, Oralene Simmons, Martha Koon Gardenhight.

The November groundbreaking celebrated a major step forward in the rehabilitation of the school, with restoration of the building's exterior set to begin.

Begining in 1947, the "Colored" children of Hot Springs had to catch a train from Hot Springs to Marshall, NC and then board a school bus with the children of Marshall to attend the Long Ridge School in Mars Hill.

Endnotes for Notable Biographies

Lillian Young Strayhorn, p. 70

1. *David Hajdu, Lush Life, A Biography of Billy Strayhorn, North Point Press, NY, back cover.*
2. *Ibid. pp. 3-5, 18.*

David Hajdu, Author and Jazz Musician, p. 71

1. *Oral Memory by Richard Dillingham, 2022.*
2. *New York Times, August 9, 1920, P. 2SR.*

Omar Lewis McClain: The Journey, p. 74

1. *Underwood, "This Is Madison County," p. 24, 1975.*
2. *Ibid., p.39; Puladen, "Victims," pp. 81-83, 1982;*
3. *Oral Tradition.*
4. *Underwood, p.25.*
5. *Ibid., p. 26.*
6. *Federal Census, Madison County, 1900.*
7. *Federal Census, Madison County, 1940.*
8. *Leonard McClain, Oral History.*

Nationally Known Rosenwald School Alumni, p. 78

1. *The Campaign to Create a Julius Rosenwald & Rosenwald Schools National Historical Park, EHT TRACERIES, Inc., pp. 39-41, 2018.*

At Rest

The Historic Mars Hill Anderson Rosenwald School

Legacy Families

Joseph Anderson Family

Over the years, Joseph Anderson Family and descendants have been members of Piney Grove and Mount Olive Churches. Joseph Anderson's grave and Jane Ray's marker are located on Joe Anderson Drive of Mars Hill University campus. Two children of Joseph Anderson and Jane Ray left descendants, Cordelia and Cornelius Anderson. Many of them are buried in the Mount Olive Cemetery.

Joseph Anderson and Jane Ray Descendants

Cornelius "Neal" Anderson, son of Joe Anderson.

Cornelius "Neal" and Frances Roland Anderson

Cornelius "Neal" Anderson, son of Joe
Frances Wilson Anderson, granddaughter-in-law
Doskey Anderson McDowell, granddaughter
Ulysses McDowell, grandson-in-law
Flora Henson Anderson, granddaughter-in-law
Oscar Young, grandson-in-law

Dallous Anderson, grandson
John Anderson, great-grandson
Octovius Anderson, grandson
Curley James Anderson, grandson
Thelma A. Young, granddaughter
Frances McDowell Briscoe, great-granddaughter

Manuel Briscoe, great-grandson-in-law
Mildred McDowell Smith great-granddaughter
Fred "June" McDowell, great-grandson

Ned Smith, great-grandson-in-law
Betty Young, great-great-granddaughter
Irene Ray McDowell, great-granddaughter-in-law

Ronald Avery McDowell, great-grandson
Ulyssis McDowell, great-grandson
Claude B. Ray, great-great-grandson-in-law
Larkwood Ray, great-great-grandson-in-law
Ned Smith, Jr., great-grandson-in-law

Catherine A.R. Singleton, granddaughter
George McDowell, great-grandson
*Pattye Ray, great-great-granddaughter
Joel Smith, great-great-grandson
Mildred Smith, great-granddaughter

Andy Anderson, Twin (died in 1870s)
Cordelia Anderson, Twin

Doskey Anderson McDowell, granddaughter of Joe Anderson.
Photo: Walter Smith

Effie Anderson Coone, granddaughter
Dillard Coone, great-grandson
Patrica Ann Coone, great-great-granddaughter

Floyd John Coone, great-grandson
Kelly Cornelius Coone Jr., great-grandson
Cordelia Coone Wilson, great-granddaughter

Gertrude Bruton Kilgore, great-granddaughter
*Oralene Graves Simmons, great-great-granddaughter

*Still Living

Viola King Barnette Family

Viola King Barnette, mother
Kathleen Williams, daughter
William H. Barnette, son
Michael Douglas Goins, great-grandson
W. Herbert Barnette, son

Shirley V. Sewell, daughter
David Barnette, son
Margaret Felder, daughter
Gregory Barnette, grandson
*Flora Barnette, daughter-in-law

*Still Living

Viola King Barnett

Remembering Homecoming

When my dad was a young man, there was always a family reunion and Homecoming for the families who originated in Yancey County, Burnsville, Barnardsville, Marshall, Hot Springs, and Mars Hill, NC.

The reunion was held on Saturday, with a gigantic picnic, visiting ancestors on the mountain of Yancey County, and family gatherings. Sunday was Homecoming—Sunday morning church, then dinner in the dining hall. There was always a visiting church, either from Tennessee, South Carolina, or Asheville and the surrounding areas. They would be the guest church for afternoon service, usually starting at 3 p.m.

During the weekend, many relatives would also visit the ancestors buried in the Mt. Olive Missionary Baptist Church cemetery and lay flowers in remembrance.

All this continued even after the closing of the school at the end of the 1964-1965 school year.

Now during Homecoming weekend, although the alumni and families have aged, and traveling has taken its toll, the school building is open once again, not as a school, but as an Interpretive Museum and Cultural Center.

~ Fatimah´ Rashida Shabazz

> Since there was not a church in the Long Ridge community, church meetings were held in the one-room schoolhouse of the Long Ridge School.

Local African American Resting Places

Piney Grove Graveyard
Walker Branch on Paint Fork of Little Ivy

During the late 1800s Blacks began to move into the Piney Grove section of Paint Fork. As the community grew there was a need for a place to worship; therefore, around 1906 Piney Grove Church was established by the Dolf Coone, Earl Connelly, Ferguson, and Anderson families.

The first church was a simple structure with a potbelly stove. The Rev. Sandy Ray of the Big Ivy Community was the church leader, and his support deacons were Harve Ray, Dolf Coone, Gilbert Briscoe, all of the Piney Grove Community except for John Ferguson of Yancey County.

Blacks began to move into Madison County, with a large population moving into a section called Long Ridge near Mars Hill. Since there was not a church in this community, church meetings were held in the one room schoolhouse of the Long Ridge School. This provided a modest place for worship but a need for a larger church grew. This being a factor, the Piney Grove Church was sold by Uncle John Ferguson for $120 and another church, Mount Olive Baptist, was built in the Long Ridge Community of Madison County.

Known graves in the Piney Grove Cemetery included Alfred Briscoe (1850-1922); Adaline Conley (1850-1935); Carolina Briscoe (1856-1923); Bowditch Ray (1865-1953); Sarah Essie Wilson, a daughter of Adaline Conley, (1875-1944); Nate Ray (1881-1933); Mark "May?" Coone (1896-1917); Nelson Ray, (1881-1918); and Addie Ray (1900-1930), with a grave marker, while all others have field stones for markers. Addie Ray was daughter of Henry and Tilda Ray.[1]

Mount Olive Baptist Church Cemetery
Long Ridge Community

The Mount Olive Cemetery was established in 1936 on land purchased from the Madison County School Board, with named Trustees as John Ferguson; Oliver Barnett; Jim Hampton; and Rev. J. H. Smith. Many years later the Mars Hill VFW Chapter erected a Veterans Flag Memorial on the old school playground adjacent to the school and cemetery. Many of the African American Legacy Families are buried there: Joseph Anderson descendants; Viola King Barnette and descendants; and many American veterans.[2]

Mount Olive Cemetery was established in 1936. Many of the Long Ridge communities African American Legacy Families are buried there. Photo by Renato Rotolo

Some African Americans are buried in the old Forks of Ivy Graveyard, at the end of Long Ridge.

Other Known African American Burial Sites

White Graveyards, Mars Hill Area

- Thomas W. Ray Family Graveyard, Gabriel's Creek, MHU (Joe Anderson's Rays)
- Ramsey Graveyard, Bruce Road, Mars Hill, NC
- Old Forks of Ivy Graveyard, about 30 graves with fieldstone markers, some Blacks buried here, Roland, on knoll above where the 1843 Fork Log Church Building stood, end of Long Ridge, above Oss Deaver home place; removed c. 1970.[3]

American Veterans, Mars Hill VFW, Flag Memorial

Claud B. "Louis" Ray, Army
Clyde James Young, Army, WWII
Ulysses McDowell, Navy/Army, Korea
James B. Hampton, Air Force, Korea
Larkwood Ray, Army
Harlon Wilson, Army
Ned Smith, Jr., Marine Corp
Michael Douglas Goins, Army
James Edward Young, Army, WW II

James R. Briscoe, Army, WWII
William Albert Ray, Army, Korea
Sherrill Roland, Army, Korea
Jerome S. Higgins, Army, WWII
Richard B. Conley, Navy, WWII
David G. Wilson, Army, Vietnam
Joel Anthony Smith, Army
William H. Barnette, Navy, WWII
Octavius Anderson, USNR, WWII

Black Graveyards, West Yancey County Area

Charlie Piercy Black Graveyard (aka Wilson Yard), at Swiss on Tomberlin Property, where Charlie Piercy (1837-1917), a Yancey County African American landowner and Free Man of Color, is buried. Each autumn, Yancey County African American family descendants return from many states for Surrogate Grave Decoration and Dinner on the Grounds.[4]

Roland Cemetery (African American)
Surnames: Flacks, Roland, Young

- "Cecil, son of A.M. and Mollie Roland, 5/14/1919-12/12/1919. Asleep in Jesus." The marker has three stars atop it.
- "John Young, d. 3/27/1904."
- "Haret Young, d. 9/24/1904. We will meet again." Same marker as John Young; foot stone also has their names.
- "Jeff Roland, d. 5/9/1908, age 77. My trust is in God." Has two stars atop headstone; name also on foot stone.
- "Lizzie Young, dau. of R. & S. Young, 5/20/1873-8/23/1903. Gone Home." On the base is the date "Nov. 1923" (perhaps when the marker was erected).

Decorated graves at the Yancey County Cemetery.
Photo courtesy of Charity Ray

Also reportedly buried here (fieldstones) are:

- James Flack and wife Sally Roland (sister of James). These are the parents of Tom Flack (d. 11/21/1972, and not buried here), and a much liked person. This may not be the following person listed on a Yancey Co. death certificate which reads: "James Luther Flack, b. 3/3/1861 in Rutherford County, NC, son of W.H. and Clarabelle Flack, died 3/15/1950, buried in the Roland Cemetery.
- James Roland, who had sons named Will (employee of Nu-Wray Inn in Burnsville) and Arseamous (moved to Mars Hill, NC).
- Millard Roland (brother of James), killed in a dynamite explosion on Jacks Creek in 1942, (along with Jess Wheeler). If I am not mistaken, his death certificate lists his age as 93 years. Millard reportedly shot Dick Young over a property squabble.

There are about 50 graves in all, almost all marked with fieldstones (some fallen down, and with the rows so crowded that it is very difficult to tell headstones from foot stones). The marked ones are concrete, hand inscribed.

Years ago, at reunions and decorations, perhaps 100 people would be in attendance, driving their cars (including Cadillacs from NY, I was told). The person who organized this was a lady named Lena Young from NY and Asheville.

The graveyard is located on Silvers Gap Road, formally known as Higgins Branch in Roland Hollow where Clint Higgins's house stands beside where the old Roland Church stood, and near where the old patriarch James Roland once lived.[5]

Remembering our Alumni and Friends

These individuals went home to Heaven in 2020 and 2021. They contributed to life on the Ridge, in the church, and at the school.

Mr. Herbert Barnette

Mrs. Louise Ray Braxton

Mr. Billy Briscoe

Mr. Tommy Briscoe

Mrs. Pauline Cheek

Mr. Edwin Cheek

Ms. Maude Gaines

Mr. Willie Henson

Mr. Eugene Jones

Mrs. Dora Wilson McClain

Mrs. Dorothy Ray Koon

Ms. Charity Ray

Mr. Preston Ray

Mrs. Sylvia Ray Stokeley

Mr. Altheston Stokeley

Ms. Edith Stokeley

Ms. Ethel Stokeley

Ms. Peggy Wilson

May They Always Rest in Heavenly Peace

The old bench from the church and schoolhouse.

Bowditch Cemetery, a.k.a. Billy Ray Cemetery

Located directly below the Billy Ray Cemetery in the Prices Creek/Cane River area.

- George Bowditch, 1844 – 2-2-1914
- Jackson Flack, 9-1878 – 6-26-1902, son of W.M. & Dullia Flack. Note: this stone was listed on the 1939-40 WPA Cemetery Survey but was not found on the 2003 survey.
- 20-25 graves marked with fieldstones.

Death Certificates

- Charlie William Wilson, emancipated from slavery, about 80 years old, died 7-14-1939; son of Charlie W. Wilson and Polly Anderson, and his wife Chaney Wilson (formerly enslaved), died July 19, 1936 at age 98 years, daughter of Charlie Stacey and Harriett Dellinger. Both certificates state "buried at Ray Cemetery."
- Death Certificate for Jennie Gardner Bowditch, died Feb. 2, 1921, age about 96, wife of George Bowditch, daughter of Jake & Mary Gardner Roland is said to be buried at Prices Creek Cemetery and thought to be buried here with her husband.
- Pollie, married but no surname listed, died April 11, 1918, age 50, daughter of Tom Percie & Jennie Gardner. According to death certificate is said to be buried at Prices creek, likely this cemetery.

Other possible formerly enslaved individuals listed as being buried at Cane River and likely at this cemetery are:

- Flora Bowditch, died Oct. 10, 1916, about 32 years old, married but no husband listed, daughter of Jim Ray & Phyllis Gardner, wife of Alf Bowditch who is buried at Horton Cemetery in Burnsville.
- Smokey Blythe, about 30 years old, Colored, single construction worker from Birmingham, Alabama, killed on July 17, 1914 by pistol shot accident.
- Nathan Ray, Black male, married, died June 6, 1916 at age 105, parents' names unknown.
- Alfred Summey, 70 year old African American widower, farmer, died Oct. 22, 1932. No parents' names listed.[6]

African Americans are listed as being buried at Cane River or Billy Ray Cemetery located in the Prices Creek area.

Manuel Briscoe Memorial Plaque

Town of Mars Hill Historic Lampposts Memorials

On North Main Street in the Town of Mars Hill, beside the sidewalk, by the MHU Day Building, under a lamppost, is the historic Memorial Plaque Marker for Manuel Briscoe, a long-time employee of the town of Mars Hill. Manuel is a Black legend of Mars Hill, the Long Ridge Community, and of Madison County.[1]

Manuel Briscoe's home, in the Long Ridge Community adjacent to the school building, is still owned by his family. He was a Deacon in the Mt. Olive Baptist Church and Gospel Music Leader of the Mt. Olive Singers. During segregated years he led the Singers throughout the White churches in the French Broad Baptist Association of Churches, influencing significant positive race relations in Madison County.[2] Also, during the critical years of integration for the Madison County Schools, Manuel served as Chairman of the Mars Hill Anderson Rosenwald School Committee, along with Arseamous Roland and Augusta Ray. Working with the Board of Education, County Commissioners, and his Long Ridge Community, Manuel was able to negotiate a peaceful integration of the schools, what the outsiders, NAACP from Asheville and others, could not, as Manuel was known and respected in Madison County.[3]

Historically, two of the strongest supporters of Manuel Briscoe and his Long Ridge Black Community have been Mars Hill University and the Town of Mars Hill.[4]

MHC President Robert Lee Moore, while also serving as Superintendent of Madison County Schools in 1905, helped to secure land and build the new Mars Hill Colored School on Long Ridge.[5] Years later, Manuel Briscoe attended that school. In 1929, again, Dr. Moore was serving as Chairman of Madison County Board of Education when more land was bought and Rosenwald monies were secured for what became the new Mars Hill Anderson Rosenwald School,[6] which Manuel also attended.[7]

Further, years later, with the leadership of MHU President Dr. Dan Lunsford, the MHARS Friends Group was organized in 2008 on the University campus, with staff members from his administration serving as members and leaders in the MHARS Friends Group, during the first ten years.[8] During that period, the University held its first public celebration at the school site during Founders Week, honoring Joe Anderson and Jane Ray as one of the Founding Families of the University. The University also funded one of the significant Rosenwald windows in the school building to memorialize Joe Anderson and his family, for whom the school was named.[9] (The new Anderson name for the school came through Manuel's wife, "Little" Frances McDowell Briscoe, great-granddaughter of Joe Anderson.)[10]

Manuel Briscoe

Manuel is a Black legend of Mars Hill, the Long Ridge Community and of Madison County.

The Town of Mars Hill also funded one of the large Rosenwald windows as a memorial to Manuel Briscoe for his long-time employment and service to the town.[11]

From the beginning, the town was a supporter of the Long Ridge School and Community. During the 1940s, MHC Dean R.M. Lee, as Mayor of Mars Hill, helped connect the community (outside the town limits) to the town water system.[12] The motivating factors for this water-line extension were the death of students at the school from typhoid fever germs that contaminated their spring water on South Main Street.[13] The town water line was extended to the north edge of the community. Later the Board of Education bought water pipes, while the men from the community dug the 2,000-foot-long ditch, bringing running water from the edge of the community to outside the school building.[14] Some years later, water lines were extended to restrooms inside.[15]

The restored windows at the school.

The Anderson name for the school came through Manuel's wife, "Little" Frances McDowell Briscoe, great-granddaughter of Joe Anderson.

The Historic Mars Hill Anderson Rosenwald School

Viola King Barnette Funeral Service

Remarks by Richard Dillingham, Mt. Olive Baptist Church, August 27, 1983

Viola King Barnett.
Photo: Susan Mullallay

Because Viola King Barnett wrote to the State Superintendent of Schools, all rural children of North Carolina have a chance to go to high school.

It is appropriate that the Funeral Service for Viola King Barnette be held on the 20th Anniversary of the now famous oration by the great Black American prophet for social and economic justice, Dr. Martin Luther King, Jr. It was twenty years ago this weekend that he proclaimed to the world: "I Have a Dream."

More than fifty years before Dr. King proclaimed "I Have a Dream," a young girl by the name of Viola King, then living on the Biltmore Estate, was baptized in the waters of the Swannanoa River into the church body of faith, as Viola recalled, "…and I saw a great light." Dr. Martin Luther King, Jr. had a dream; but Viola King saw a vision!

The vision from that great light followed her through life from the waters of the Swannanoa River to beside the humble stream of Gabriel's Creek in Madison County, North Carolina. The vision of that great light brought protection, hope and dignity to her living.

Before the 1940s, Viola's children and other Black children of Madison County and rural North Carolina did not have access to a secondary education. Being the law that all children attend school until age sixteen, Viola wrote the State Superintendent of Schools in Raleigh and asked that Madison County Black children be able to attend high school. The Superintendent answered her letter, saying: "Because of your letter, all rural children of North Carolina will have a chance to go to high school." I still hear her happy voice: "…all the children of North Carolina!"

Twenty years ago, Dr. Martin Luther King, Jr. prophesied from Washington, "I Have a Dream," but more than fifty years earlier, Viola King saw the dream! Because of her, friends and neighbors in Madison County have also seen her dream; children of Viola King Barnette, you, too, have seen the dream. Earlier this year, Mama's photographic portrait and story toured the state of North Carolina in the exhibit: "Hope and Dignity." This month, Temple University Press published Mama's story in *Hope and Dignity: Older Black Women of the South,* so that the whole world can now know of the great light!

Children, grandchildren, and great-grandchildren, forever, tell your children to tell their children that Mama "saw a great light," and her living has blessed us all.

The Scriptures teach: "…and they shall rise up and call you blessed!"

Viola King Barnette, your friends and neighbors, we rise up and call you blessed; your brothers and sisters rise up and call you blessed; your children, they too, rise up and call you blessed; and, "All the children of North Carolina," for them, we too, say blessed!

Charity Ray Obituary

Blue Ridge Funeral Service, Mars Hill, NC, 2020

Charity Ray was born on June 1, 1937. She was called home to begin her heavenly journey on October 2, 2020. Charity was the daughter of John and Augusta Briscoe Ray and sister to Dorothy Ray Coone and Christina Ray Rucker, all of whom are deceased.

She is survived by her loving nieces Linda Rogers of Dalzell, SC and Connie Overcum of Morristown, TN, as well as a host of great- and great-great-nieces and nephews.

Charity was a fifth-generation resident of the greater Mars Hill area. Her family first lived in a log cabin near the present Ingles grocery store in Mars Hill, later building their home in the Long Ridge Community. Charity and her sister Dorothy resided in their parents homeplace before passing.

She attended the Mars Hill Anderson Rosenwald School in the Long Ridge Community and graduated from Allen High School for Girls in Asheville. After graduating from high school, she moved to New York City and worked for some years before returning home to help take care of her sick father.

In 1970, Charity began working at Mars Hill College as a secretary, later becoming a staff member in the curriculum lab and Renfroe Library, where she retired with more than thirty-eight years of service.

Charity always held a great love and devotion to Mt. Olive Baptist Church. As a member, she was the church pianist, and along with her uncle Manuel Briscoe, she helped organize the Mt. Olive Singers. They performed gospel music in churches throughout Madison County. "In that way, we made many friends in Madison County," she said.

Charity was an excellent cook and enjoyed helping Mt. Olive Baptist Church hold its annual fish fry. She was also featured in *Our State* magazine for her famous apple stack cake!

Charity's love for art and painting "was a gift, it wasn't anything I learned," she said. She began her art at age five at the Mars Hill Rosenwald School where the teacher allowed her to "doodle" as Charity described it. In retirement, she joined the weekly meetings of the Church Mice art group in Mars Hill. Her watercolor paintings have brought pleasure to many near and far.

Charity worked to help rehabilitate the Rosenwald School Building where her art began. As an alumna, she served as a member of the Friends Group and member of their History Committee.

She also had a great love for plants and flowers and watching them grow. In her last years, she received great pleasure in feeding and observing her "wild friends," the birds, squirrels, turkeys, and deer, feeding in her back yard.

Charity was also blessed to have two guardian angels, Flora Barnett and Richard Dillingham, while here on earth. Their friendship and devotion showed true Christian love. In addition to Flora and Richard, the family would also like to thank the many residents of Mars Hill for keeping a watchful eye on Charity, everyone is truly appreciated.

A graveside service was held Wednesday, October 7, 2020 at Mt. Olive Baptist Church Cemetery.

Charity Ray

Charity worked to help rehabilitate the Rosenwald School Building where her art began.

Many members of the African American Legacy Families are buried at Mount Olive Cemetery, including Joseph Anderson descendants and Viola King Barnette and her descendants.

Endnotes for at Rest

Local African American Resting Places, pp. 84-89

1. Vickie Anders Sealock, "Addie Ray grave marker research: Piney Grove Black Graveyard," native of Paint Fork, I-26 West NC Welcome Center Manager, NC Welcome Center, located on Listen B. Ramsey Freeway, in Madison County, NC; Madison County Heritage Book, Vol. I, p.32; Dan Slagle internet information, 2022.
2. Joseph Anderson Community Celebration Program, Long Ridge Community, October 13, 2010.
3. Richard Dillingham Community Research Notes, "The Forks of Ivy."
4. Elaine Dellinger, Yancey County local historian, cemetery research information by phone, August 5, 2019.
5. Elaine Dellinger & Gwen Bodford, 4/16/2002, Shared 2/15/22.
6. Ibid., 2019, shared 2/15/22 & 4/15/2022 (Yancey County Black Death Certificates); Dellinger: Yancey County DAR Member and author of Lost Cove & Its People, 2022.

Manuel Briscoe Memorial Plaque, p. 90

1. Town of Mars Hill: North Main Street, Lamppost Beside MHU Day Hall, Town Files, 2002.
2. Pauline Cheek Interview with Manuel Briscoe, 1984 and Teresa Buckner Interview with Charity Ray, "MHC Employee Reflects on Changes," 2009.
3. Madison BOE Minutes, 1963-65, extracted by Pauline Cheek and Dan Slagle.
4. MHU, Joe Anderson Memorial Window, MHARS Minutes. TOMH Manuel Briscoe Memorial Window, MHARS Minutes.
5. Madison BOE Minutes, 1905.
6. Dan Slagle research, "NC Directory of School Officials for Each School Year... Internet Archive Site," 1929-30.
7. Edwin B. Cheek Interview with Manuel Briscoe, 1983.
8. Ophelia (Fifi) DeGroot Notes, Dillingham Notes, MHARS Friends Group Minutes, 2008-2022.
9. MC Education Foundation income records.
10. Joe Anderson Kiosk, MHU campus (Doskey McDowell's Daughter, "Little" Frances).
11. MC Education Foundation income records.
12. Madison BOE Minutes.
13. Pauline Cheek Interview with Manuel Briscoe, 1984. Oral Tradition: Augusta and Charity Ray. Holcombe Funeral Home records, MHU Archives.
14. Madison BOE Minutes, 1940s.
15. Ibid., 1950s.

Preservation

The Historic Mars Hill Anderson Rosenwald School

Support Sought for Historic Schoolhouse

by Loretta Atkins, from The Hilltop, *the student newspaper of Mars Hill College, 2008*

Because school segregation is a thing of the past, it can be easy to forget that Blacks and Whites used to receive educations in completely different locations.

> The Long Ridge/Anderson School was the main school for Blacks in Mars Hill from 1905 until school integration finally came in the 1960s.

Although legally integration began in 1954, some areas, including Madison County, were slow to accept it.

The Joe Anderson School, located on Long Ridge in Mars Hill, was one of the many schools that educated Black students who were not allowed to attend the White schools. Though it has long been in a state of disrepair, efforts are being made to restore and preserve it as a historic landmark.

The present building was financed by Julius Rosenwald (1868-1932), who made his fortune as president and leader of Sears, Roebuck and Company. He donated millions of dollars to have schools built for African Americans in the South, including nearly 900 schools in North Carolina alone.

According to the State Department of Cultural Resources, the Long Ridge/Anderson School here in Mars Hill is the only Rosenwald School remaining in the mountain counties of the state. Several others in the eastern part of North Carolina have been restored and are now historical monuments.

The Long Ridge/Anderson School was the main school for Blacks in Mars Hill from the 1920s until school integration finally came in the 1960s. Since then it has fallen into disrepair and even been used as a tobacco barn. Volunteers from the college and from Mars Hill Baptist church have discussed joining in a cleanup; however, the structure itself is somewhat dangerous.

"There is so much history with this school. It's one of the few all Colored schools left. This school is a big part of Mars Hill community. The history and the community tie together," says Stuart Coates of Mars Hill Baptist's In-As-Much volunteer group. Coates is also director of emergency management in Madison County. "The individuals that live there (in the Long Ridge neighborhood) have done a lot and helped out a lot of people in Madison County. There are a lot of ties back through that community."

Charlene Ray, who graduated from Mars Hill College in 1981, wrote a research paper that year titled "The History of Blacks in Madison County: 1860-1981." In it she said:

> "The Joe Anderson Elementary School in Mars Hill was the main educational center for Blacks in the Mars Hill area after the 1920's. This school only went to the sixth grade. After that, Blacks in the county were either fortunate enough to be sent to a boarding school like Allen School in Asheville, or they were forced to quit. Sometime in the 1930's, after agitation by such people as Viola Barnette, the State Superintendent of Education decided that funds would be allotted for Blacks to be bused from Mars Hill to Asheville to the Black high school there, Stephens-Lee. The State and Madison County also provided funds for two teachers to teach at the Elementary School instead of one. At one time there were sixty-five Black students at the Joe Anderson Elementary School being taught by one teacher."

Reprinted with permission of MHU and author.

Our Story, This Place

The Long Ridge/Anderson School in 2008, still standing tall, but in desperate need of repair.

The significance of the Long Ridge/Anderson School in the history of Mars Hill became a subject of discussion recently when the owners of the property that lies out past the school asked the Madison County Board of Education to give them a right of way so they could demolish the school and widen the road for a new real estate development. The board hired a survey company to find out exactly what they owned.

"They saw the school as more than just a building there. They didn't want it torn down," Coates said. Although they did not have the money to do the many repairs that the building will need, they voted as a Board not to let the landowners have a twenty-foot right of way, Coates said.

The hope is to restore the building, then give it to the Mount Olive Baptist Church across the street that serves the neighborhood. "We've met with them, and they have open arms and are willing to take it. After it is redone and fixed up, they want to make it like a community building. Meals and birthday parties and things like that can be held there. Like a little community center," Coates said.

The building itself has been added to, but the plan is to save the original building. If money can be raised, an architect would be hired to come in and actually do the blueprint of the building. There is some wood that would have to be replaced; some can be re-used. According to Coates, a person in the community has come forward and is willing to work with the Long Ridge group (people in the community) and write a grant to get money to redo the building.

The School Board is considering "stabilizing the building" with a new roof to prevent further deterioration while plans are developed to find funding for renovation.

So far, clean-up work by volunteers has only been done outside the building. According to Craig Goforth, who is both a member of the school board and dean of student life at the college, students will not be recruited to work inside until the school board is satisfied that the building is safe.

According to a survey that was done in August 1965 by Madison County Schools, Anderson Elementary School was acquired in 1927. It had a floor area of 1,632 square feet and was located on 1.1 acres. It held grades 2-6, and was heated with coal-fired heaters.

Coates added, "That community is aging out, and we would like to do something for them. There's a lot of history and a lot of people that have ties back out through there that now live in far-off places, yet they still come home. We want to keep the memory alive."

According to the North Carolina Department of Cultural Resources, the Long Ridge/Anderson School in Mars Hill is the only Rosenwald School remaining in the mountain counties of the state.

Reprinted with permission of MHU and author.

The Mars Hill Rosenwald School Rehabilitation Project

The school in 2010

The movement to save the Long Ridge school building began when Stewart Coates of the Madison County Board of Education recommended that the building not be torn down, but given back to the Long Ridge Community for preservation. Some years later, the movement continued with the "In-As-Much" Mission Group of the Mars Hill Baptist Church. Rev. Justus, Edwin and Pauline Cheek, Stewart Coates, Dr. Lee, and others organized activities for saving the school building. In 2008, Richard Dillingham made a presentation to the Rotary Club that encouraged them to help with the preservation. His history presentation was taken from Edwin B. Cheek's research in 1983: "Arts and Crafts in the Long Ridge School," which Professor Dillingham had supervised at the college.

Also, in 2008, Phyllis Stiles introduced Dillingham to Margaret Newbold and Barry Williams with the Conservation Trust of North Carolina in Raleigh. Thus, the first meeting was called for December 16, 2009 on the campus of Mars Hill University. Those attending were: Stewart Coates, Ed and Pauline Cheek, David and Willa Wyatt, Fifi DeGroot, O'Neal Shelton, Phyllis Stiles, Richard Dillingham, and others. Stewart Coates was elected Chair of the Friends Group and Standing Committees were established: Building and Grounds; Finance and Grants; Alumni; and History. The next meeting was scheduled for March 12, 2010, with Margaret Newbold and Barry Williams attending.

Margaret Newbold, Associate Director of Diversity, Conservation Trust of North Carolina from Raleigh, along with Barry Williams, Diversity Project Coordinator, met with the Friends Group. Newbold's grandfather, Nathan Carter Newbold, had been Director of the NC Division of Negro Education with the NC Department of Public Instruction. Viola King Barnette's letter would have gone to Director Newbold.

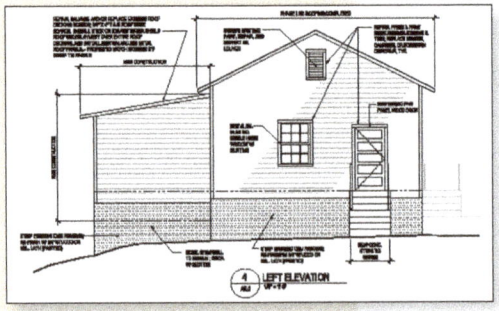
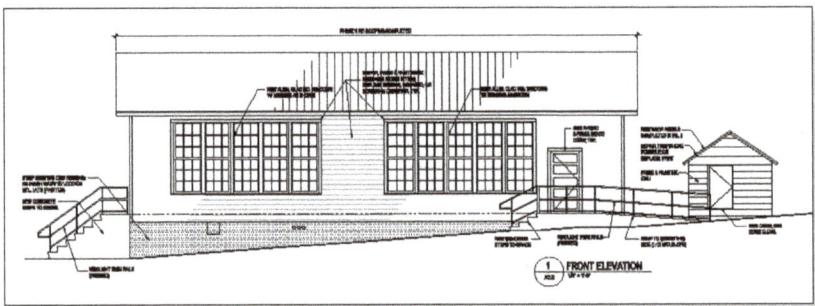

Plans for restoring the historic Anderson Rosenwald School provided by Architect Scott Donald of Padgett & Freeman Architects.

The first public gathering, celebrating the Long Ridge Community and the Rosenwald building rehabilitation took place in October 2010 as part of Mars Hill College Founders Week, celebrating Joe Anderson, for whom the Anderson Elementary School was named.

Also during 2010, Willa Wyatt was elected chair of the Planning Committee, as she and husband David Wyatt had been members since the beginning. Architect Scott Donald, Padgett & Freeman Architects, rendered the drawings for the rehabilitation of the historic building, meeting preservation standards for historic preservation, as the Mars Hill Rosenwald school building was placed on the State Study List for possible listing in the National Register of Historic Places.

Long Ridge neighbor Simone Bouyer, Ad World Services, became Webmaster for the Friends Group. Theresa and Ryan Phillips, Legacy Films, Ltd., are Media Specialists for the project. Fatimah´ Shabazz, who attended the school, agreed to be Chairwoman of the Alumni Committee. Members of the History Committee were Charity Ray and her sister Dorothy Coone, both having attended the school; Pauline Cheek; Richard Dillingham; and later, Dan Slagle.

During 2010, monies were secured from the Conservation Trust of North Carolina and the Madison County Board of Education to place a new roof on the building.

In 2011, students from Elon University filmed interviews of alumni and friends of the school for an eight-minute video on the Rosenwald School, now posted on the website. Also Mars Hill University students from Lifeworks and Bonner Scholars programs rendered community service for the school project. In fact, they received the National Award for the best photograph during the National Martin Luther King Day of Service in 2012, for their work on the Rosenwald school property. The winning project photograph was captured by their religion professor Dr. Marc Mullinax.

In 2013, Friends of the Mars Hill Anderson Rosenwald School completed its Strategic Plan with the leadership of Judy Futch and Paul Smith of Judy Futch Counsulting, Inc. The rehabilitation project qualifies for tax-deductible gifts under the Madison County Education Foundation.

In September 2014, the Rural Heritage Museum at Mars Hill University opened its exhibit, "Our Story—This Place. The History of African American Education in Madison County, North Carolina: The Mars Hill Anderson Rosenwald School." Les Reker, former director of the museum, is a member of the Friends Group.

In November 2015, the Rehabilitation Ground-breaking Program was held at the school site with a large group of friends, supporters, and alumni in attendance.

In 2018, the historic school building was placed on the National Register of Historic Places, and a rehabilitation grant for $50,000 was received from the National Trust for Historic Preservation, one of only eleven in the nation.

In 2019, the building rehabilitation progressed to a Grand Public Dedication during Homecoming Weekend in the Long Ridge Community and Mount Olive Baptist Church, August 30 – September 1, 2019.

Today, there are other Rosenwald buildings still standing, having used the free Rosenwald building plans, including the Rock School Buildings in Madison County. The Mars Hill Anderson Rosenwald School, according to the Fisk University Rosenwald database, is the only funded Rosenwald School still standing in Western North Carolina, and is the only known Rosenwald School still owned and operated by a public school system in North Carolina, or even in the South.

The rehabilitated Long Ridge Community's Mars Hill Anderson Rosenwald School is designed to serve as a Community Cultural Center, an extension of the Madison County School System, and an Interpretive Museum, so as to promote a fuller understanding of Southern Appalachian Black history in the Blue Ridge Mountains, and to enhance education at all levels.

Mars Hill University students working to clean up the grounds at the school. This photo, taken by Dr. Marc Mullinax, won Best Picture for Dr. Martin Luther King Jr, Day of Community Service in 2012.

Mars Hill University students who volunteered to clean up the grounds at the school.

The Historic Mars Hill Anderson Rosenwald School

Friends Group Planning Committee Members and Contributors

In December 2009 an initial planning group convened to explore how to preserve the Long Ridge Community Anderson Rosenwald School.

Willa Wyatt has led the Friends Group committee for more than 10 years.

Over the years, numerous individuals, including students from Mars Hill University, have been instrumental in planning for the future of the school.

Lakia Allah	Scott Donald	Jane Maney	Inez Ray
Judy Balsanek	Darlene Dunn	Lori Hagen Massey	Preston Ray
Flora Barnette	Hank Dunn	Cleveland Martin	Bishop William Ray
Herbert Barnette	Justin L. Derr	Sandy McCall	A.D. Reed
Kevin Barnette	Scott Donald	Omar McClain	Les Reker
Donna Beavers	Jameson Donnell	Annie McDonald	Beth Ross
Terry Bellamy	Phillip Michael Ervin	Justin Metcalf	Lenny Ross
Gordon Benton	Ciara Felder	Julia Moore	Fatimah´ R. Shabazz
Karen Blevins	Judy Futch	Tracy Morgan	O'Neal Shelton
Russell Blevins	Steve Garrison	Ben Morrell	Carol Shields
Wallace Bohanan	Doneisha Gartica	Kaye Myers	Oralene Simmons
Darhyl Boone	Norris Gentry	Margaret Newbold	Dan Slagle
Kasey Boston	Forrest Gilliam	Mark Norwood	Pat Smith
Simone Bouyer	Augusta Gladding	Aerial Odan	Paul Smith
Colie Brown	Andy Gregg	Samantha Odham	Walter Smith
Teresa Buckner	Sarah Weston Hart	Arlene Pettway	LaHalica Snyzeen
Jan Caldwell	Jeane Hoffman	J. Bruce Phillips	Maia Surdam
Jennifer Cathey	Will Hoffman	Ryan Phillips	Jonnee Taylor
Edwin Cheek	Neeczi Jackson	Theresa Phillips	Katie Terry
Pauline Cheek	Barbara Jones	Shirley Pike	Sandra Tolley
Bud Christman	Eugene Jones	Wesley Pike	Caroline Twiggs
Stewart Coates	Tommy Justus	Lawrence Ponder	Michael Wallin
Jessie Coleman	Karen Kiehna	Alexis Poplos	Oscar Weston
Dorothy Coone	Joy Kish	Travis Proffitt	David Wyatt
Charles Cutshall	Howard Lee	Christiaan Ramsey	Willa Wyatt
Joe Davis	Page Lee	Dorothy Rapp	Bob Zink
Melissa Dean	Max Lennon	Ray Rapp	
Fifi DeGroot	Ruth Lennon	Alonzo Ray	
Richard Dillingham	Dan Lunsford	Charity Ray	

What the Anderson Rosenwald School in Mars Hill Has Meant to Me

Letter from Stewart Coates

Volunteers helped clear the grounds around the school building in 2010.

During my tenure as the Chairman of the Madison County Board of Education many items came before me which required hard decisions but few as painful as the Anderson Rosenwald School building. Yes, an old wooden building set off the beaten path but still owned by the Madison Board of Education. A school building with deep, deep roots which need to be told. A school building tycoon [John D. Rockefeller, Jr.] visited around 1922. He later funded an art room that helped change the lives of many. But no one saw this old building for what it used to be because now all they only wanted was to tear it down in order to widen the road to support a few homes.

The destruction of the Anderson Rosenwald School was not going to happen on my watch. I wanted to know more about the building and its history. The building was in disarray with the roof falling in on the back side, windows were broken out and the door was wide open. Large trees had grown up touching the roof and trash had been dumped around the building. It was time to act. It was time for help. This building still had a purpose and a story to tell.

I heard stories about how young children played hide-and-seek in the old school building. Another story told about a group of children who played basketball inside the building to get out of the rain. But the one story that stood out was how the building was turned into a barn to dry burley tobacco. Throughout all the years the old building still stood, and stood tall with a story to tell.

It was time to act and so many did. The first task was to clean up so we could see what we had. Mars Hill Baptist Church holds a fall event each year called "In As Much." Cleaning up around the old building became one of their projects. I called Michael Boone, a local business owner, to cut down the big trees. The old building started to take on new life but everyone knew it was going to take a lot of money, time, and resources.

As I began talking to several people, things started to come together. Two key people were Willa and David Wyatt. With David's contacts and knowledge, a plan was made on what we would need moving forward. Several small meetings were held in conference rooms at Mars Hill University and Mt. Olive Church to organize a formal committee to bring the Anderson Rosenwald School building back from the ruins to life. Willa was the co-chair for the committee and it was amazing how she was able to get everyone involved at all levels. I feel that the Anderson Rosenwald School would have failed if not for Willa and David Wyatt.

Thank You,
Stewart Coates

Several meetings were held at Mars Hill University and Mt. Olive Church to bring the Anderson Rosenwald School building back to life.

Scott Donald

With more than 32 years with PFA Architects, Scott has planned and delivered several of the firm's largest and most complex projects. Scott has lived all over the United States as the child of a military family, settling in Asheville in 1990. He became partner in 1998 focusing on educational, commercial, and institutional facilities, most recently serving as Partner in charge of A-B Tech's Ferguson Center for Allied Health and Workforce Development.

Architect Scott Donald

With his thorough understanding of project management and construction administration, Scott is adept at navigating complex projects with clear communication and promoting cooperation between the owner, contractor, and design team. Professional collaboration, exceptional project delivery, and a sense of humor are the standard in Scott's work.

Scott holds a Bachelor of Architecture from Louisiana Tech University and NCARB Certification. In his free time you can find him camping, hiking, or raising rescued shelter dogs.

Members of the Friends of the Mars Hill Anderson Rosenwald School

David and Willa Wyatt (Madison County Schools – retired)
Ed and Pauline Cheek, (Mars Hill College – retired; deceased)
Will Hoffman (Madison County Schools)
Scott Donald (Padgett and Freeman Architects)
Fatimah´ Rashida Shabazzz (alumna)
Omar L. McClain, Jr. (alumnus)
Richard Dillingham (Mars Hill University – retired)
Charity Ray (Mars Hill College – retired, Anderson School alumna; deceased)
Dorothy Coone (Anderson School alumna; deceased)
Kevin Barnette (Mars Hill University, son of Anderson School alumnus)
Lenny (Long Ridge Community) and Beth Ross (deceased)
Russell Blevins (Mountain Valleys Resource Conservation & Development Council)
Travis Proffitt (Mars Hill University)
Kasey Boston (Mars Hill University)
Ciara Felder (MHU student)
Doneisha Gartica (MHU student)
Justin Derr (MHU student)
Steve Garrison (Madison County)
Simone Bouyer (web designer, Long Ridge Community)
Stewart Coates (Madison County Schools)
Fifi DeGroot (Mars Hill University – retired)
O'Neal Shelton (Madison County Rotary Club)
Becca Johnson (NC Dept. of Cultural Resources)
Kaye Myers (NCDCR)
Margaret Newbold (NC Conservation Trust)
Teresa Buckner (Mars Hill University)
Oralene Simmons (alumna)
Eugene Jones (alumnus; deceased)
A.D. Reed (Helen Tarasov Reed Memorial Fund)

Friends of the Mars Hill Anderson Rosenwald School

Friends of the Mars Hill Anderson Rosenwald School, 2011.

Leaders: Stewart Coates; Willa Wyatt

Secretaries: Fifi DeGroot; Teresa Buckner; Simone Bouyer; Lauren Rayburn; Judy Balsanek

Alumni: Fatimah´ Shabazz

Building And Grounds:
David Wyatt, Willa Wyatt, Dan Slagle, Scott Donald, Padgett & Freeman Architects, Jimmy Willis, MH Hardware, JAS LLC

Fundraising/Grants:
David Wyatt; Willa Wyatt; Lauren Rayburn

History: Richard Dillingham; Dan Slagle, Sarah Hart, Charity Ray (deceased); Dorothy Coone (deceased); Pauline Cheek (deceased)

Media: Theresa Phillips, Legacy Films, Ltd., Ryan Phillips, Cinematographer; A.D. Reed, Publisher

Webmaster: Simone Bouyer, Ad World Services

MHU Representatives: Fifi DeGroot; Joy Kish; Ray Rapp; Les Reker

Strategic Planner: Judy Futch & Paul Smith, Judy Futch Consulting, Inc.

Historic Preservation: Jennifer Cathey, Restoration Specialist, State Historic Preservation Office, NCDR, Western Office

Work Volunteers (Building & Grounds): Dan Slagle, Coordinator; Justin Metcalf; David Wyatt; Willa Wyatt; Ben & Jesse Wyatt; Fatimah´ Shabazz; Omar McClain; Charity Ray; Ray Rapp; Dorothy Rapp; Les Reker; Wallace Bohanan; Philip Ervin; Bill Zink; Ryan Phillips; Richard Dillingham; MHU Students; Mark Norwood

2011 Rosenwald Scholars

These Mars Hill University students participated in the rehabilitation project.

Kaley Kite – Outreach and Volunteer Coordinator Fellow

Traci Jo Morgan – Education Fellow

Nichole Brown – Media and Public Relations Fellow

Jonee Taylor – History and Rehabilitation Fellow

Katie Terry – History and Rehabilitation Fellow

The Long Ridge Community Anderson Rosenwald School

The interior of the school in 2021.

Mission

The Mars Hill Anderson Rosenwald School, located in the Long Ridge Community, will serve as a Community Cultural Center and Interpretative Museum, intended to promote a fuller understanding of the Rural Highlands of Southern Appalachian Black history and to enhance education at all levels.

Vision

The vision of the Long Ridge Community Anderson Rosenwald School is to preserve this school and its story—"Our Story, This Place"—as a living heritage of southern Appalachian rural Black history.

Strategic Plan 2013–2016

Strategic Planning Process

After several years of discussion and planning, the Long Ridge Community Anderson Rosenwald School Planning Committee decided develop a strategic plan to guide the restoration activities of the Long Ridge Community Anderson Rosenwald School during 2013–2016. A Strategic Planning Committee, comprised of the committee chairs, met to identify the strategic directions and broad goals needed to develop the School. Through a participatory process, the Planning Committee developed the vision and guiding principles to guide the organization. A draft plan was developed by planning consultants and reviewed by the Strategic Planning Committee and the Planning Committee.

Strategic Planning Agreement

The Long Ridge Community Anderson Rosenwald Project Planning Committee approved the strategic plan in March, 2013. The plan represents the commitment of the Planning Committee to the mission, vision, guiding principles, and organizational goals and objectives that they defined during the planning process. The Planning Committee recognizes that active governance, oversight, and participation are required to fulfill the goals and achieve the mission and vision. The volunteers are committed to developing well-defined action plans, monitoring the plans, and adapting as needed to fulfill the strategic directions outlined in this plan.

~ Willa Wyatt, Chair, representing the Long Ridge Community Anderson Rosenwald Planning Committee, March 8, 2013

History

Julius Rosenwald, part-owner and president of Sears, Roebuck and Company, established the Rosenwald Fund in 1917 for "the well-being of mankind." The largest project of this fund, undertaken with input and encouragement from African American educator Booker T. Washington, involved providing funds for African American schools throughout the American South.

Between 1917 and 1932, the Rosenwald Project provided over $4.4 million in matching funds for over 5,000 schools plus teachers residences and shop buildings in fifteen states. The schools were constructed according to models designed by architects at Tuskegee Institute in Alabama to maximize light and ventilation.

The Long Ridge Community Anderson Rosenwald School (previously known as the Mars Hill Colored School and as the Long Ridge School), located in the Long Ridge community of Mars Hill, NC, was one of those 5,000 schools. The school was completed in approximately 1930 with funds raised by the Mars Hill African American community and the Madison County Board of Education, with additional funds from the Rosenwald Project.

More than 2,000 African American children from Madison County attended the Long Ridge Community Anderson Rosenwald School during the years it operated. The school closed in 1965 as a result of integration, and Madison County School system continued to own the building. The Historic Anderson Rosenwald Rehabilitation Project has a memorandum of understanding with Madison County School system regarding the use and care of the school building and site.

Progress to Date

In December 2009 an initial planning group convened to explore how to preserve the Long Ridge Community Anderson Rosenwald School and continued meeting in 2010. The Planning Committee met monthly from 2011 to 2013. The activities below reveal primary steps the Planning Committee has taken:

2010 – Initial rehabilitation plans for The Long Ridge Community Anderson Rosenwald School building were developed by an architect; subcommittees were established; Elon University created a film and conducted four interviews with alumni; a mission statement was drafted; roof rebuilt; trenches dug for electric lines; Mars Hill University students hired as "Rosenwald Scholars"; trail maintenance conducted; website developed, Community Celebration event held on October 13, 2010

2011 – Financial support received from North Carolina Conservation Trust; building renovations continued; Planning Committee networked with a state and regional preservation groups, Madison County officials, Madison County School system, and local community groups

2012 – Historical research about the school continued; building restoration continued; oral history interviews conducted; Community Block Grant presented to the Madison County Commissioners; application made to the Department of Housing and Urban Development; strategic planning process begun; oral history interviews continued; mission statement approved

---

It is estimated that more than 1,500 African American children were educated here, attending the Long Ridge School (1905-1928) from Mars Hill and attending the Anderson Rosenwald School (1929-1965) from Madison County, a 60-year period of Black education at "This Place."

The Historic Mars Hill Anderson Rosenwald School

Historical research on the school continues.

The school can currently host students and study groups.

Strategic Directions 2013 – 2016

In the next three years, The Long Ridge Community Anderson Rosenwald School would enhance and expand relationships with community stakeholders to ensure that the following strategic directions are reached:

Preserving the Long Ridge Community Anderson Rosenwald School

The school building is a place where the community can gather and programs can be held.

Educating the community about the Long Ridge Community Anderson Rosenwald School

Through educational programs, people in the Blue Ridge region understand the impact of the Long Ridge Community Anderson Rosenwald School on the Black community and on the community as a whole.

Reaching out to Madison County and surrounding counties

People in Madison County and surrounding counties work together to ensure that the Long Ridge Community Anderson Rosenwald School is sustainable and accurately represents the students, families, and communities surrounding the Long Ridge Community Anderson Rosenwald School.

Ensuring longevity of "our story, this place"

Long Ridge Community Anderson Rosenwald School has organizational structures and policies in place to ensure capacity to provide programs.

Our Story, This Place

Greetings from Madison County Schools

From Superintendent Will Hoffman

The Mars Hill Anderson Rosenwald School is a beautiful, living example of history—one that allows us, even forces us, to have an honest view of the nation's history—in particular your history as alumni and their descendants. Rooted in a legal system of segregation that unraveled many of the gains of the Civil War and Reconstruction, the school brings to life our nation's struggle to live up to its original ideals while serving as a reminder of our flaws.

Nationally and in North Carolina, social studies standards are at the center of discourse that is often controversial and layered heavily along political lines. Members of state legislatures claim that if we talk honestly about our history our children will be harmed by learning that, for generations, we fostered a racial caste system of inequality. But what happens when those with the power to tell our history are challenged? When those previously ignored demand to be heard? Can we ask hard, uncomfortable questions about our nation's past without being viewed as unpatriotic?

I want our graduates from Madison County Schools to understand and be proud of our history and feel that they have the power to contribute to that rich story. MHARS will be a valuable means to address the state's social studies standards and our teaching of North Carolina history, hosting student field trips, faculty professional development, and community events. The school will function as a lens on the past to teach our students about our local history and culture, the history of education in America, and the realities of segregation and the fight against it.

The Madison County Board of Education appreciates the incredible work of the Alumni and Friends of the Mars Hill Anderson Rosenwald School. As Superintendent of Madison County Schools, I have been truly impressed by the dedication this group of alumni and friends of MHARS have shown for the past twelve years. Now their work is nearing completion, and our school system is eager to work with the Friends of MHARS in any way we can to fulfill our shared goals.

Superintendent Will Hoffman

A ribbon-cutting ceremony was held to celebrate the school's rehabilitation in 2019.

Our Story, This Place
Exhibit at the Rural Heritage Museum

The Historic Mars Hill Anderson Rosenwald School

Our Story, This Place

Historic artifacts, including a chalkboard, school desks, and teaching aids, were included in the exhibit.

In September 2014 the Rural Heritage Museum at Mars Hill University opened the exhibition: "Our Story, This Place—The History of African American Education in Madison County, North Carolina: The Mars Hill Anderson Rosenwald School."

Historic artifacts, including a chalkboard, school desks, teaching aids, and a reconstructed privy were placed on display. The exhibit was on display through February 2015.

Welcome!

I am Fatimah´ Shabazz. My mother, Mrs. Mary H. Wilson, was a teacher at the Mars Hill Anderson Rosenwald School (MHARS) for 14 years, 1939-1953.

To save time, when I was four, mom decided to take me with her to school; this was a better choice for everyone. This versus her driving me across town five days a week to deliver me to my grandmother's and then drive to Mars Hill to teach.

As I gained a little age, being a smart-aleck child, thinking I knew best for me, on a few occasions, I would say to my mom, "I am going to run away." She would respond, "Okay, but first get a good education." Those words

Fatimah´ Shabazz stands in front of the school's historic piano during rehabilitation. In 1938 Fatimah´s mother, Mrs. Mary Wilson, recommended to the Madison County School Board that they purchase a piano for the school. They agreed that they would spend $10 for a piano from Dunhams Music House in Asheville, but teacher and community must pay the remainder monthly. The piano shown above is that historic piano!

supported me through college, my career in California, locally, and to this day.

Participating with the Friends of MHARS Committee, I have learned and discovered histories I was totally unaware of, in addition, learning of families and family connections in the Long Ridge Community—all while being the Facilatator of Communication for Alumni & Families.

For you, we choose that you enjoy and embrace a most unique history, 'Our Story, This Place' and participate with us in the evolutionary process of MHARS.

Our Story, This Place

The Mars Hill Anderson Rosenwald School Exhibit at the Rural Heritage Museum

by Les Reker, Director, Rural Heritage Museum, Mars Hill University

Today's historians tell us that a *sense of place* is what defines a people. This exhibition then, tells the story of African American education in a place called Mars Hill, Madison County, North Carolina. It details the history of a people's experience, in their own words, from Reconstruction through the period of integration and the Civil Rights legislation in the 1960s.

The Long Ridge School, later the Mars Hill Anderson Rosenwald School, played a significant role in the history of African American education in western North Carolina. In this exhibition, aspects of the day-to-day learning experience of the students who attended the school are featured. The exhibition also reveals some of the struggles, the hopes and dreams of their teachers and their parents, in the context of the time. All of this is presented through the experiences of students who attended the school. The legacy of the Rosenwald education on their adult lives is also presented. Every effort has been made to secure and present a factual picture of events in this story. Research in this area continues.

As a visitor to this exhibition, we hope that you take away an educated awareness and a greater understanding of the struggles and success stories experienced by African American families in their desire to provide a quality education for their children in Madison County after Reconstruction. Another goal is to provide an opportunity to understand the hope for a brighter future that the Mars Hill Anderson Rosenwald School provided African American children between 1929 and 1965.

The panels and materials included in the exhibit will be part of a permanent display at the Mars Hill Anderson Rosenwald School.

Exhibit History Panels written by Richard Dillingham except Introduction Panel by Les Reker and "Legacy" Panels by Oralene Simmons.

Reprinted with permission of MHU's Rural Heritage Museum.

The Historic Mars Hill Anderson Rosenwald School

A Pioneering School for Black Children in Madison County Finally Gets Its Due

A Rural Heritage Museum exhibit in Mars Hill honors the Rosenwald School, a historic African American school in Madison County.

Written by Cameron Huntley, *Mountain Xpress, January 23, 2015*

If you wander off the beaten path in Mars Hill, you might come to a dead end on Mount Olive Drive in the community of Long Ridge, not far from the town's university. There sits a solitary building that appears forlorn and somber, at first.

A peek inside reveals fragments of green tile still clinging to the floor and chalk graffiti decorating the walls. There's a chimney, sturdy as ever, and evidence of pipes that likely ran to coal stoves. A pale line runs up the length of the chimney, as if a wall once stood there and neatly bifurcated what's now just one big room.

The building seems inauspicious, until you peer into its legacy: In fact, this humble structure is a rare standing relic of the Jim Crow South and a monument to how Madison County's small but vibrant Black community carved out its own education for generations. And now, the former school, which has gone by a few names over the years, is finally on the verge of getting its proper recognition, a once-fading legacy now coming back into focus.

A boon and a challenge

It's a history that dates back to the Civil War era. After their emancipation, many former slaves stayed around Mars Hill and built new lives. "There were other areas settled by African Americans in Madison County," says **Les Reker**, director of Mars Hill University's Rural Heritage Museum, which is helping drive new interest in the school. "But Long Ridge was the area predominately settled by African American families."

Black migrants from less peaceful locales swelled the numbers. "Madison and Yancey used to be one county," Reker recounts. "Their split may have actually been because Madison was more pro-Union, and Yancey more Confederate. Many African Americans moved to Madison from Yancey County because the Ku Klux Klan was so active in Yancey."

A few small, spread-out schools sprang up to serve Black children, and in 1905 many of these coalesced into a centralized one called Long Ridge School by the students (and Mars Hill Colored School by White school boards). This facility did the job until 1930, when it was replaced by the Long Ridge Rosenwald School, the product of a pre-desegregation push to radically improve academic options in places like Mars Hill.

Funds to build the school came from a grant of $750 (about $8,000 in today's dollars), matched by the community and school district. The grant came from the Rosenwald Fund, which was the brainchild of Julius Rosenwald and Booker T. Washington. The former was a wealthy philanthropist and admirer of the latter.

Washington believed that self-help and education among African Americans was the best means of improving their communities, and that after a period of improvement, they could challenge inequality by force of their economic viability and social indispensability.

Omar McClain and Fatimah´ Shabazz.
Photo by Pat Barcas

Reprinted with permission of **Mountain Xpress.**

Rosenwald, a part owner and top executive of Sears, Roebuck and Co., took the notion to heart, and with Washington launched a grant program that funded African American schools. By 1932, when the last of them was built, close to 6,000 Rosenwald schools stood throughout the South, 800 of them in North Carolina alone.

The qualifications for receiving a Rosenwald grant were simple: The building had to match Rosenwald specifications (the foundation provided many potential building plans; Mars Hill used Plan 20, according to Reker), and the community and school district had to furnish part of the funds.

Starting in 1930, all African American students in Marshall started being sent and ultimately bussed to the Long Ridge Rosenwald School. This was the situation when **Omar McClain**, a Marshall native, attended from 1950 to '54.

"I'm one of those people that caught that little yellow 10-passenger bus," McClain says. "They would come and pick us up from Marshall, and I didn't really realize … the sacrifice that [the bus driver] made—the driver was one of my classmates. If I had to get up at five in the morning, what time did he have to get up? 'Cause he had to drive all the way to Marshall and back."

The school taught eight grades in two classrooms: first to fourth in one, fifth to eighth in the other. The teacher "was juggling all these people at the same time," says McClain. "Each grade would have their own stuff." Younger kids sat in front, and the teacher started the mornings with them. "They'd do their little thing, and then she'd move onto the next."

Preserving history

In 1965, with the advent of integration, the Long Ridge Rosenwald School (known since 1959 as Anderson Elementary) closed for good—11 years after *Brown v. Board of Education of Topeka, Kansas,* declared segregated public education unconstitutional.

The Madison County school system maintained ownership of the building, but no one seemed sure how to use it. It served as a sometime recreation center, basketball court and even a tobacco barn, but nothing lasted, and for decades the building just sat there as nature moved in to claim the husk that remained.

Perhaps it would have stayed on this path until it completely disintegrated. But in 2003, a neighbor wishing to expand a road that passed by the school from his property asked the Board of Education to demolish the building. The board refused, and a long conversation ensued about what to do with it.

In 2009, an informal committee of school alumni formed with an eye on preserving the school in some fashion. As the push grew and other community members joined, it became the Friends of the Mars Hill Anderson Rosenwald School in 2011. With help from volunteers, the group began clearing the property of debris and making repairs to the building.

"They are rehabilitating it, not restoring it," notes Reker. "To 'restore' it means returning it to its original use. That can't happen, for obvious reasons." Rehabilitation, however, still means that the building, to garner governmental protections, must look exactly as it did before, right down to the materials used; the few exceptions are modern features such as handicapped access and air conditioning.

Efforts to preserve the Rosenwald School in Madison County have been unflagging. The exhibit in Mars Hill told the story of how the Rosenwald School—built in 1928 and later named Anderson Elementary—served the African American community in the area.

Photo courtesy of the Rural Heritage Museum

Reprinted with permission of Mountain Xpress.

The Historic Mars Hill Anderson Rosenwald School

Fatimah´ Shabazz, right, and Omar McClain were students at the former Rosenwald School. A Rural Heritage Museum exhibit in Mars Hill honors the school.
Photo by Pat Barcas

When the rebuilding is complete, organizers say they may turn the facility into a full-fledged community cultural center—but whatever form it takes, it will be one that forever preserves and shares the story of how Black students and teachers persevered in separate and unequal times.

Of course, there is much work remaining before that can happen. At present, it's estimated that $130,800 is still needed to finish the project, including new windows, siding, floors, wiring, paint and HVAC.

But publicity and support for the effort have been growing, bolstered most recently by Reker's historical efforts and a series of panels on the school, hosted by Mars Hill University and featuring many of the Rosenwald School's alumni. In September, the university's Rural Heritage Museum opened an exhibit, *Our Story—This Place*, devoted to African American education in Madison County and using the former school as a focal point.

"It became apparent," says Reker, "that this was a very important, yet largely unknown, story that occurred right here in Western North Carolina."

The exhibit, which will remain open through the end of February, houses numerous school artifacts, and massive panels feature blown-up photographs and facsimiles of many newly discovered documents pertaining to the school. "These documents reveal the decision making that occurred over the years with regard to segregation," says Reker.

Perhaps the most significant excerpt of a public record on display reads, in part:

Madison County Board of Education Meeting, June 1, 1964 9:30 p.m. …

Action: *Consider Geraldine Griffin's written request to place her Child in the Mars Hill "White" School?/Consider requests by other parents.*

Action: *Approved*

School days

In extensive interviews with *Mountain Xpress*, four of the school's alumni recounted in detail just what it was like to attend their Rosenwald School.

Dorothy Coone and her sister, **Charity Ray**, lived nearest, in Mars Hill part of the time—during which their father usually drove them to school—and then in Long Ridge, at which point they walked. McClain, as mentioned, took the bus from Marshall. **Fatimah´ Shabazz** was from Asheville, and attended the school because her mother, **Mary Wilson**, was a teacher there.

Wilson ended her teaching career in 1953 as a 14-year veteran of the school; close to an entire generation learned in her classroom, where she taught grades one through four. "It was kind of like she was on roller skates," McClain recalls. "She didn't do much teaching from the desk."

The older students, says Ray, were there to help out if Ms. Wilson was occupied. The atmosphere was ever orderly, Coone says. "You didn't really have any disturbance in the room, even with four different grades."

Reprinted with permission of Mountain Xpress.

And if there was any misbehavior? "We got two different degrees" of discipline, McLain says with a laugh. "She'd do your hand with a ruler if you did something minor. But if you broke the cardinal rules or something, she had a little Bolo bat. She'd bend you right over them chairs and bust you right out there. It wasn't … violent, or even painful. But the embarrassment was unbelievable. You'd cry just because you were embarrassed."

"It was either a switch or ruler when we went," says Coone. "Girls didn't get switched," Ray adds, smirking.

There were three rooms in the building. A parlor "where we hung our little cloaks," says Shabazz, and the two classrooms. In the center, on the windowed side, was a brick chimney. A sliding partition ran from the chimney to the other wall, separating the classrooms. Two pot-bellied coal stoves were connected to the chimney, one in the corner of each room. One student was designated "fire-keeper," responsible for lighting the stoves before school started and feeding them coal throughout the day.

Down below the school was an outdoor privy, which served as the restroom until the school got plumbing in the late 1950s. There was one spigot outside that all the kids used to wash their hands.

School started at 8 a.m. and went until 3 p.m. Lunch was around noon, with recess right after that. Each day, Shabazz says, began the same way: "You come in, hang up your coat, sit down and have devotion—singing a song, reciting a scripture by memory and doing the Pledge of Allegiance."

The coursework was very much up to the discretion of the teacher. Students learned the basics—reading, writing and arithmetic—but McClain recalls other lessons catered to local living conditions. "Our curriculum dealt in the world," he says. "We had studies on leaves and vines … what you could grab or not grab, what to eat or not eat. Most people lived off the land … and I think that it contributed mightily to the longevity of the people."

One of the obstacles to learning was the state of the classroom materials, books in particular. The school couldn't afford new books, nor did the school system provide them, so all books were secondhand, with some in better shape than others. "We didn't get any new things at all," says Coone. "And part of the book would be there, and the other part wouldn't." Shabazz recalls getting hand-me-down texts from public libraries. "Whatever kind of books we could get, we read," she says.

Ironically, the students' lack of access to standard reading materials sometimes ended up exposing them to more-challenging works. "There was Shakespeare, all that," Shabazz says. Shakespeare, in the first grade? "Yes," she insists, laughing. "Not only did we read it, but we acted them out."

Ms. Wilson "was big on classroom participation," says McClain, as if performing Shakespeare as an eight-year-old were the most normal thing in the world. "Acting it out," Shabazz continues, "you really can relate more to what you're reading."

Connecting community

Acting practice and plays the students put on for the community were a big part in a big school tradition, say alumni. Holiday and end-of-year plays were standard, though often there were others throughout the school year, often to fund a class trip or other activity.

"It was an efficient way to raise money for something," says McClain. The teachers would slide back the partition, and "all the community would come—White, Black, whatever. It would be packed with people."

One student was designated "fire-keeper," responsible for lighting the pot-bellied coal stoves before school started and feeding them coal throughout the day.

Reprinted with permission of **Mountain Xpress.**

Former students Fatimah' Shabazz, center; Omar McClain, left; and museum director Les Reker, right. Photo by Pat Barcas

"The whole neighborhood [came]—sometimes people your parents worked for, [and] even people from uptown [Mars Hill]," says Coone.

Many of the productions were in the Nativity vein, especially around holidays like Christmas and Easter. Others were shorter, more like skits.

"I remember one of them we did," says Coone. "It was about hats."

"It was 'hats, hats, hats,'" Ray reminds her, replicating the hand motions accompanying each utterance.

"We got out Mother's hats—the ugliest one," says Coone. "I also remember one play: we were supposed to be daisies. We had on white dresses our mothers made, and they made the hats out of construction paper. … And we had a choir, so we'd sing."

"Ms. Wilson had a knack for getting the word out," says Ray. "She could really get people to come."

"It was kids that put on the play, but it was a community effort," says Shabazz. The tight-knit local neighbors played a huge role in the lives of the students. "The community raised the children as much as the parents," she says. "When we got out of school, we didn't have to worry about going home. If nothing else, we went to someone else's house until someone was home to meet you. Safety and security was big."

"All the families knew each other," Coone says. "Most families were large, had eight or nine children. I think we were the smallest group with just three girls."

"Everybody knew everyone's comings and goings," says Ray. "It was a way of protecting one another."

"When I was a kid, I actually thought everyone on that ridge was related to us," says McClain, "because the trust was there. I remember, both my parents were working at the time, and I stayed with this White family at the house next to me," he adds. "But they cared about me."

Racial matters

All four alumni describe a relatively peaceful racial situation in Mars Hill and the surrounding countryside, even as the Civil Rights movement ramped up in the 1950s.

"The people who lived near me, there was never that racial thing going on," says McClain. "It just wasn't that way at that time. When my grandmother's house burned down in Marshall, the next day, Black and White, they were rebuilding that house. They just jumped in."

Virulent racism "wasn't a pertinent way of being" in that part of Madison County, Shabazz remembers. "The mindset of the community [was] it didn't really matter. Everybody took care of everybody else."

"Mostly it went well," Coone says of the racial dynamic. "You might have some people, but they usually wouldn't let you know. The Blacks here wouldn't have stood for it. They'd let you know right then what they thought and it would never come up again. To me, the smaller town is better because everyone knows each other. Half the time, their parents grew up with your parents."

Reprinted with permission of Mountain Xpress.

Ray, describing interactions with White school-age peers, says: "If you got the best of them, they started getting nasty, so you just clobber them one. It didn't mean your friendship would end tomorrow—you'd play together again, but the name-calling wasn't there anymore." Still, she says, "Our playmates would ask our parents why we couldn't go to school with them."

"I think it had to do with the economic level," says McClain of the state of Black-White relations. "It was basically the same. We were all on the same level. No one could point down to you."

Both McClain and Shabazz hint that there was a certain feeling of normality to the situation—that segregation was just the way things were, and thus went unquestioned. "When we were in school, there was no time devoted to racial disharmony," says Shabazz. "They did teach us about Booker T. [Washington] and Frederick Douglass," says McClain. "At the time, we thought there was only two Black men who ever did anything."

"I don't think any of us knew the history of that school (Rosenwald) or how it all came about," Shabazz adds.

"It was always there," says McClain. "My mother went to that school. We just all thought it was always there."

But even if Mars Hill was relatively accepting and safe, the kids were schooled in a segregated setting and could not escape the broader cultural landscape. "I knew racism existed," says McClain. "Because every now and then someone would holler out a window or something. When we traveled, or pulled up in a diner, we couldn't go in the front and eat, we had to go around and get the food to go, where people would wash the dishes or whatever."

Shabazz in particular has a unique perspective on racial matters during her childhood. As a native of Asheville, she attended the Rosenwald School with an outsider's view to the interactions in Mars Hill; she, too, contends that it was "a little different" in the rural community.

Mars Hill "didn't carry that torch as much," says Shabazz. "In the city [of Asheville]? Yeah. I was aware of the lack of respect around my mom and dad, which really upset me as a child."

Indeed, no matter how ideal Mars Hill was or wasn't, it only took a half-hour trip south to the Land of the Sky to find the indignities.

Major department stores and other locales, they recall, were particularly problematic, and the memory got a rise out of McClain. "Let's don't go there. White and Black water fountains."

"White and Black bathrooms," says Shabazz. "Yep. And where Diana Wortham is, there used to be a theater called the Plaza, and we went in on Market Street."

"Around the corner to go in," says McClain.

"Up to the balcony," says Shabazz. "And then we'd throw things down on your heads."

During high school, meanwhile, most Madison and Buncombe county African American students attended Stephens-Lee in the East End neighborhood of downtown Asheville (Coone and Ray both attended Allen, a private high school for African American girls, also downtown).

African American students from Madison had to do this because there was no Black high school in Madison County. For a long time, those students had no option to go to high school at all—Stephens-Lee was, after all, way out of district.

And before North Carolina raised the mandatory age for school attendance to 16, with no high school for them, this meant that many Black children in Madison who finished 8th grade at the Long Ridge Rosenwald School would simply have to repeat the 8th grade over and over until they turned 16.

> **"I don't think any of us knew the history of that school (Rosenwald) or how it all came about."**

Reprinted with permission of **Mountain Xpress.**

The Historic Mars Hill Anderson Rosenwald School

Mars Hill native **Viola King Barnette** was instrumental in getting this changed—so much so, Reker says, that she's considered a "crusader for Black education." King, a domestic worker whose son **Herbert** attended the Long Ridge School, wrote the North Carolina Department of Education to request that schoolchildren from the Long Ridge school be bused to Stephens-Lee after 8th grade. The state superintendent responded in the affirmative, paving the way for McClain and many other Madison natives to attend high school when they otherwise wouldn't have been able.

McClain and Shabazz both light up when speaking about their time at Stephens-Lee.

"[Lee Edwards High] were our rivals," says Shabazz. "We used to kick their butts in football."

"And when they had the [holiday] parade, our band was the toughest around," says McClain.

"Man, our band was *bad*," says Shabazz, meaning they were "so [awesome] that initially we used to be up front or in the middle [of the parade]; but people would just start leaving [after we passed], before Santa Claus came!"

"So they put us at the end, to make everybody stay," McClain adds.

"I remember being on Asheland Avenue one day," says Shabazz. "And this gentleman was chewing tobacco, and he did this *ptch-chew* spitting kind of thing, and he said 'I ain't leaving till Stephens-Lee gets here.' You can check the history, but it happened: Our band brought in Santa Claus, because [otherwise] people would leave."

"I had a good time at Stephens-Lee," she continues. "At Asheville High? No."

Shabazz is the only one of the four that experienced integration while still in school. She spent her senior year at the new Asheville High School, which integrated Lee Edwards and Stephens-Lee. It would prove to be her least-favorite year of schooling. "Our class was the first to have integrated teachers," she says. "And a lot of teachers at Stephens-Lee lost their jobs. "All highly educated, all had Masters [degrees]."

"They didn't want to take a pay cut," says McClain. "And rightfully so: they had degrees, why should they have to take a pay cut?"

"I know I went to a meeting in Asheville," says Ray. "And they were discussing equal rights, and these were supposed to be educated people. They weren't from way out [in the country]. And one lady says, 'You all just have to give some of us time to love you.' And I said to her, 'Your love is not worth a dime. What we want is equality. When we go to work someplace, we want to get paid equally.'"

Ray pauses a moment, thinking. "I guess that lady has grandchildren by now. Maybe she learned to love or something. But I didn't hold it against her. I don't think she realized what she was saying."

Homecomings

All four Rosenwald alumni left western North Carolina after their schooling, and all eventually made their way back.

McClain joined the Army after graduation. After leaving the service, he moved to New York, embarking on myriad enterprises: "I went to college there, worked on Wall Street, owned an inventory business, and at the end I owned a nightclub." But tiring of the "rat race," McClain says, he returned to western North Carolina in 2008.

After her tumultuous senior year at Asheville High, Shabazz migrated to the West Coast. "I swore I would never come back," she says. She lived in California, Virginia, and Atlanta, for the most part keeping her distance from her hometown. In 1993, she had to return to take care of her parents, arriving just when the infamous blizzard hit. "It's like God was saying, 'You ain't going nowhere,'" she recalls.

All four Rosenwald alumni left western North Carolina after their schooling, and all eventually made their way back.

Reprinted with permission of **Mountain Xpress.**

The Ray sisters departed as well. Charity wound up in New York. After working there for several years, she returned home to take care of her ailing father, and stayed. She got a job at Mars Hill College (now Mars Hill University) as a circulation assistant in the campus library, a position she kept for 39 years.

Dorothy went to Virginia, working for a bank as a credit analyst. After her husband passed away, she returned to Mars Hill to help take care of her mother, and she, too, decided to settle. The sisters live together in the house they moved into in the 1940s, the one that made it possible to walk to school.

All four have been intimately involved with the rehabilitation campaign. When it started, Ray recalls, "We said, 'This school is still standing.'"

"Separate but equal" was always a lie, but that just makes the quality of education in the Rosenwald School all the more remarkable.

"When we went to Asheville schools from Mars Hill schools, there was this thing like we aren't supposed to be ready, because we came from a rural school," McClain remembers. "But most of the teachers were vested in our future, either by relationship or family. It seemed like they put a little more into it to make sure each person was prepared. We were more than ready."

Cameron Huntley, "We Remember: Saving Madison County's Rosenwald School," Mountain Xpress *(reprinted with permission), Vol. 21, No. 26, January 21-27, 2015; Front page & pp. 9-13.*

Cameron C. Huntley Obituary

Cameron Chase Huntley, 26, a resident of Nairobi, Kenya, formerly of Asheville, NC, died Wednesday, June 1, 2016 in Nairobi, Kenya.

Born April 27, 1990 in Asheville, NC, Cameron was a 2008 graduate of Erwin High School and a 2011 magna cum laude graduate of Clemson University. After college, he worked in Human Resources for the City of Asheville and was a freelance writer for the *Mountain Xpress*. He visited Kenya in 2013 with NewSpring Church of Anderson, SC, and felt called to return to Kenya in 2015.

While in Nairobi, he taught English, participated in missions and continued writing. His entire life was devoted to those in need. Cameron had a huge heart for people who were less fortunate. He lost his life protecting someone he loved.

Remembering Cameron Huntley

From Les Reker, Director, Rural Heritage Museum

"I knew Cameron Huntley as an impressive young man and incredible writer. I first got to know him when he contacted me regarding his writing a couple articles for the *Mountain Xpress* about exhibitions at the Rural Heritage Museum at Mars Hill University. One very important story he wrote was printed on January 21, 2015. It was the cover story that week. The headline was "We Remember, Saving Madison County's Rosenwald School." The exhibition about it was titled 'Our Story-This Place, The History of African American Education in Madison County, North Carolina: The Mars Hill Anderson Rosenwald School.'

"Cameron carried out incredibly extensive research for this article. He visited the Museum several times and conducted interviews with all the principle people. He also attended the panel discussions, committee meetings, and all the programing related to the exhibition. He went above and beyond what most would think was necessary for a single article. He demonstrated a deep commitment, a profound sensitivity, incredible patience, and a real passion for accuracy. Although he was writing prose it seemed like poetry....

"He was a very special person and his loss is keenly felt!"

Reprinted with permission of Mountain Xpress.

Local and National Recognition

The Historic Mars Hill Anderson Rosenwald School

Why Does This Place Matter?

The school in 2013.
Photo by Emily Chaplin,
courtesy of WNC Magazine

School Reformed

A historic schoolhouse for African Americans in Madison County finds a new community role.

In the Jim Crow era, African Americans attended separate and decidedly unequal schools throughout the South. However, some Black students received a major boost in the 1920s when philanthropist Julius Rosenwald, president of Sears Roebuck and Co., launched a fund to build new schools for Blacks in rural areas.

By the time the program ended with Rosenwald's death in 1932, there were 5,000 Rosenwald Schools in the South. North Carolina had about 800, the most of any state. When public schools were largely desegregated in the 1960s, most of the Rosenwald Schools were effectively abandoned.

Madison County's Anderson Rosenwald, an elementary school built in 1930, is one of the few remaining relics of the effort. Before it closed in 1964, some 2,000 students had been taught there.

Reprinted from WNC Magazine, *July 21, 2011*

This place, the Mars Hill Anderson Rosenwald School and the Black Long Ridge Community are historic symbols of National, Southern, State, and Local American Racial Progress in Black Education and Black Community Development.[1]

Julius Rosenwald, a White Jewish American businessman inspired by his friendship with educator Booker T. Washington of the Tuskeegee Institute, established Rosenwald Partnership Grants for over five thousand Black schools, ten thousand Black libraries, and thousands of Black teacher grants nationally. His Rosenwald Partnership Grants paid one-third of the costs; states paid one-third of the costs; while the county and community would pay the one-third balance of the costs.[2] The Mars Hill Anderson Rosenwald School in the Long Ridge Black Community was only one of the Rosenwald Schools built in the North Carolina mountains, but the only one still standing, having been rehabilitated.[3]

The majority of these Rosenwald Partnerships were established in the South, and the largest number of state Rosenwald Schools were built in the state of North Carolina.[4]

This place has the only known Rosenwald School in the South named for a former slave in Madison County, NC named Joseph Anderson,[5] who with his family helped establish the school, teach in the school, attend the school, and administer the Mars Hill Anderson Rosenwald School, and helped rehabilitate the building for a Black Educational and Cultural Center in the rural Highlands of Southern Appalachia.

- Joe Anderson served as School Committeeman in 1896, and again 1907.[6]
- His granddaughter Effie Anderson Coone taught in the Mars Hill Colored School in 1901.[7]
- His son "Neal' Anderson served as School Committeeman for the Long Ridge School in 1905-07.[8]
- His nephew Sam W. Anderson, by brother Lewis, taught in the Long Ridge Black School, 1905-07; 1911-13.[9]
- His grandson Dallas "Dowell" Anderson served as Rosenwald School Committeeman in 1953.[10] (He and wife "Big" Frances and sister Doskey McDowell worked for Mars Hill College in its cafeteria during the 1940s, 50s, and 60s.)[11]
- His great-grandson-in-law Manuel Briscoe served as School Committeeman 1960-64, as Chairman during integration.[12]
- His great-great-granddaughter Oralene Anderson Graves attended the school 1949-53; Dr. Oralene (Anderson Graves) Simmons helped rehabilitate the school building, 2014-2022.[13]
- The Anderson name was given to the school by the 1960s.[14]

Our Story, This Place

The school in 2021.
Photo by Ryan Phillips

The MHARS is the only funded Rosenwald Program School still standing in WNC, still owned and administered by its founder, the Madison County, NC Board of Education.[15]

At this place, the Long Ridge School building hosted the founding of Mount Olive Baptist Church, and caused the settlement of the Long Ridge African American Community, south of Mars Hill, NC.

Viola King Barnette, parent at this school, and washerwoman at MHC, wrote the NC Superintendent of Schools, requesting access for her children to high school. His letter in reply stated: "Because of your letter, all children in NC will have access to higher education."[16]

Augusta Briscoe Ray, alumna of the Long Ridge School, was the only known Black female to serve as Rosenwald School Committeewoman, 1953-64 for Madison County.[17] (She was mother of Charity Ray and Dorothy Coone, members of the Rosenwald School's History Committee.)[18]

This Rosenwald school building has been rehabilitated by Black and White friends and neighbors of its Friends Group, 2008-22.[19]

This place was listed on the National Register of Historic Places in 2021.[20]

This Historic Mars Hill Anderson Rosenwald School has published its notated history, "Our Story, This Place," 2022.

The Mars Hill Anderson Rosenwald School has an active alumni organization with alumni locally and nationally, and with their living descendants throughout the nation.[21]

The Historic Mars Hill Anderson Rosenwald School

The Madison County Board of Education Members and Principals read the Resolution for the Anderson Rosenwald School in November 2018, honoring the 90th Anniversary of the school.

Resolution by the Madison County Board of Education

Resolution by the Madison County Board of Education honoring the 90th anniversary of the Mars Hill Anderson Rosenwald School, upholding the core values of public education, and strengthening an educational environment free from discrimination and harassment

WHEREAS, in 1928, the Madison County Board of Education built a new school building on Long Ridge, using funds from the Rosenwald Fund for building African-American schools in the South.

WHEREAS, today, the Madison County Board of Education celebrates the historical and cultural significance of the Mars Hill Anderson Rosenwald School, which was created out of segregation at that time, and which served as a consolidated elementary school for Madison County African-American school children, serving a generation of Madison County children and standing as a beacon for 90 years on Long Ridge in Mars Hill.

WHEREAS, it has been 64 years since *Brown v. Board of Education of Topeka,* the landmark 1954 U.S. Supreme Court ruling that separate schools for African American and white children were "inherently unequal."

WHEREAS, ten years after the *Brown* decision, Congress passed the Civil Rights Act of 1964, thereby prohibiting segregation in public schools and outlawing discrimination based on race, religion, sex or national origin.

WHEREAS, despite the Supreme Court's ruling in *Brown* and the adoption of the Civil Rights Act of 1964, children in our country are still subject to and affected by discrimination and bigotry.

WHEREAS, discrimination, bigotry and hate speech in the school setting has an overwhelming negative impact on students' emotional health and well-being, as well as their ability to freely benefit from the many educational opportunities provided.

WHEREAS, our students have the basic right to attend school in an environment that is safe, promotes personal growth, volunteerism and is free from, discrimination, bigotry, and disruption.

WHEREAS, the Board of Education acknowledges the dignity and worth of all students and employees and strives to create a safe, caring, and inviting school environment to facilitate student learning and achievement.

WHEREAS, the Board of Education, and its staff, honor the history of the Mars Hill Anderson Rosenwald School and are fully dedicated to the education and support of **ALL** students, and uphold the core values set forth in Title VI of the Civil Rights Act of 1964 which provides for equal educational opportunities for all and prohibits discrimination on the basis of race, religion, sex or national origin.

NOW, THEREFORE, BE IT RESOLVED by the Madison County Board of Education:

1. That, on its 90th anniversary, the Board honors the Mars Hill Anderson Rosenwald School and the significant, historical role it played in our community for over a generation; and

2. That the Board honors the Mars Hill Anderson Rosenwald School teachers, whose purpose was to ensure African-American children in our community received a sound education despite the hardships they encountered.

In further recognition and honor of the Mars Hill Anderson Rosenwald School's 90th Anniversary, the Board further resolves that:

1. We all must strive, harder than before, to provide each of our students the opportunity for an excellent education free from discrimination, harassment and bigotry;

2. As the Board of Education's anti-discrimination policy states, we will not tolerate any form of unlawful discrimination, harassment, or bullying at school, athletics, school programs, or school events;

3. We must lead by example and demonstrate by our conduct that we are committed to equality;

4. We also must encourage and support all students to achieve their best; and

5. We want our students to leave our school district not only with strong academic and vocational skills, but also with the understanding that all people are worthy of respect and dignity.

Read and Adopted, this 9th day of November 2018.

_____ _____
Dr. Theresa Banks, Chair   Mr. Kelby Cody, Vice-Chair

_____
Mrs. Lori Hagan Massey, Member

_____ _____
Mrs. Barbara Wyatt, Member   Dr. Will Hoffman, Superintendent
                             Ex-Officio Secretary

*Three Madison County colored schools in the Mars Hill area began in the 1880s: Mars Hill; Bull Creek; and Ivy Colored schools. In 1905, the Madison County Board of Education, under the leadership of Superintendent R.L. Moore, bought an acre of land for a new school house, consolidating the Mars Hill colored elementary schools on Long Ridge, south of Mars Hill. This new school house was the beginning of the Long Ridge African American community in Mars Hill, with Black residences and Mt. Olive church to follow.

> **We must lead by example and demonstrate by our conduct that we are committed to equality.**

The Mars Hill Anderson Rosenwald School was named to the National Register of Historic Places in 2018.

Mars Hill Rosenwald School National Registry

North Carolina
State Historic Preservation Office
Department of Natural and Cultural Resources
Office of Archives and History
Division of Historical Resources

Recent North Carolina Listings in the National Register of Historic Places

Mars Hill School
Mars Hill, Madison County
https://files.nc.gov/ncdcr/nr/MD0253.pdf

Mars Hill School's construction was possible because of the Rosenwald Fund, which provided architectural plans and matching grants that helped build African American schools from Maryland to Texas fbetween the late 1910s and 1932, including 818 projects in North Carolina. Mars Hill School was the only school in Madison County assisted by the Rosenwald Fund and is one of only three Rosenwald schools known to be extant in the westernmost counties of North Carolina. The school served elementary school students in grades one through eight in Mars Hill, Marshall, and parts of Yancey County to the east and thus is significant for its association with African American education in Madison County and western Yancey County from its construction in 1928 to its closure in 1965 following desegregation. The building is a modified example of Floor Plan No. 20 in Samuel L. Smith's Community School Plans, Bulletin No. 3. Despite alterations and a loss of material integrity largely due to changed use and deterioration, the school, which is undergoing a thorough rehabilitation, retains distinctive characteristics of the two-teacher school plan and building form. The nomination for Mars Hill School was funded by an Underrepresented Community Grant from the National Park Service.

The National Register of Historic Places is the nation's official list of buildings, structures, objects, sites, and districts worthy of preservation for their significance in American history, architecture, archaeology, and culture. The National Register was established by the National Historic Preservation Act of 1966 to encourage historic preservation initiatives by state and local governments and the private sector and to ensure, as a matter of public policy, that properties significant in national, state, and local history are considered in the planning of federal undertakings. In North Carolina, the National Register program is coordinated by the State Historic Preservation Office in the Office of

NC DEPARTMENT OF
NATURAL AND CULTURAL RESOURCES

For more information, please contact Jenn Brosz
at 919-807-6587 or jenn.brosz@ncdcr.gov.
Visit our website at www.hpo.ncdcr.gov.

**State of North Carolina
Department of Natural and Cultural Resources
Office of Archives and History**

This is to certify that

**MARS HILL SCHOOL
Mars Hill
Madison County**

has been entered in

THE NATIONAL REGISTER OF HISTORIC PLACES

by the
United States Department of the Interior
upon nomination by the State Historic Preservation Officer under
provisions of the National Historic Preservation Act of 1966 (P.L. 89-665).

The National Register is a list of properties "significant in American history, architecture, archaeology, and culture – a comprehensive index of the significant physical evidences of our national patrimony." Properties listed therein deserve to be preserved by their owners as a part of the cultural heritage of our nation.

*Deputy Secretary, Office of Archives and History
and
State Historic Preservation Officer*

May 31, 2018
Date Entered

Ongoing renovation efforts aim to establish the site as an interpretive museum.

The Historic Mars Hill Anderson Rosenwald School

Rosenwald School's National Registry Now for All to See

A developer seeking a wider right of way in the early 2000s nearly led to the demolition of the Mars Hill Anderson Rosenwald School, where generations of Black students were educated from 1905-1965.

by Chance Thweatt, from the 2021 Madison County Visitor's Guide, published by The News-Record & Sentinel *in Marshall, NC*

During segregation, the Anderson Rosenwald school educated more than 2,000 African American children from Madison County. It closed in the spring of 1965. It was last used as a burley tobacco barn for years until 2009, when in order to preserve the school, the Friends of the Mars Hill Anderson Rosenwald school began the process of preserving the school.

"We began with one major goal in mind and that is to be entered in the National Register of Historic Places," said Willa Wyatt, chairman of the Friends of the Mars Hill Anderson Rosenwald School group.

On April 16, 2021, the Mars Hill Anderson Rosenwald School, located in the Long Ridge Community, mounted its building plaque about the National Register, acknowledging all the research, planning, and work that took place prior to being placed in the National Registry on May 31, 2018.

"This is a great honor because of the history and sacrifices that some of the students had to make just to attend the school because of segregation," Ray Rapp, a member of the Mars Hill Anderson Rosenwald School Rehabilitation Committee, said.

"The plaque is very special because this is the last Rosenwald school in Western Carolina," Ray Rapp said.

According to the National Trust for Historical Preservation, the number of Rosenwald Schools remaining from the 5,357 built between 1917 and 1932 is less than 500.

"Mr. Rosenwald funded over 5,000 African American Schools in the south. The White community had to raise a third of the school cost, as well as the Black community, and then Rosenwald would put his money in it," Ray Rapp said.

Between the years of 1912 and 1932 Rosenwald Schools were built across the south to educate African Americans. The schools were built under a collaboration with Booker T. Washington and Julius Rosenwald, president of Sears-Roebuck. The group's goal is to make it as close to the original building as possible.

Rapp says preservation of the school is very important because the history of the Rosenwald schools is not very well-known. The goal during the rehab was to make it as close to the original building as possible. Dorothy Rapp, the wife of Ray Rapp, has also been instrumental in the rehabilitation process.

"When we started the project over 10 years ago, the building was falling apart and we had to work really hard to get the original building cleaned up," said Dorothy Rapp, also a member of the Rosenwald School Rehabilitation Committee.

Dorothy said that it has been a step-by-step process because every Rosenwald school had a standard design.

Reprinted with permission of the News-Record & Sentinel.

Our Story, This Place

"There was a plan for all these schools. They have to be facing North and South because it was pre-electricity. When the sun came up you were getting the morning sun, and in the afternoon you would be getting the afternoon sunlight," Dorothy said.

In addition, the interior had to be a certain color all the way down to the brick of the building. The building had to look at a certain way in order for Rosenwald to fund the school, Dorothy said.

Although the school is closed to the public as of now, the committee is putting everything in place to open it up to the public.

The goal is to keep the school room portion of the school very similar to the original. The second room in the school will be more modern and include technology so school groups can come in," Dorothy Rapp said.

One of the goals of the rehabilitation committee is to use the building to bring individuals together, as well as bring awareness to all the Rosenwald Schools.

"The Madison County School Board has already had one meeting here so they could see the progress of the school. The plan is for the school board to have one meeting in the Rosenwald school once a year," Ray Rapp said.

"One of the projects that this group has done is to interview as many people as they have been able to locate, who went to school here," Ray Rapp said.

Oralene Anderson Grave Simmons was one of the people who went to school in the Mars Hill Anderson Rosenwald School.

"I am so proud to have this plaque. I think we are very deserving of this honor. I am so happy that I will be able to point it out to family members and friends," Oralene Anderson Grave Simmons said.

Simmons is looking forward to seeing the school evolve into a cultural center for education and also looks forward to seeing the historical tours that will highlight the rich culture of the Mars Hill Anderson Rosenwald School.

Ongoing renovations to the school will see it used as a living museum. Paul Moon/The *News-Record & Sentinel* [Marshall, NC]

Reprinted with permission of the News-Record & Sentinel.

In 2018, the school was placed on the National Register of Historic Places.

The number of Rosenwald Schools remaining of the 5,357 built between 1917 and 1932 is less than 500.

"Simmons is the great-great-granddaughter of Joseph Anderson, a slave who was used as collateral for an outstanding debt to build Mars Hill College in Mars Hill, North Carolina in 1856," Ray Rapp said.

Dr. Simmons, a native of Western North Carolina, has been recognized internationally as a lifetime Civil Rights leader. Simmons is also the founder of Asheville's annual Martin Luther King, Jr., Prayer Breakfast.

"I am also in the process of writing a book about my life journey, it will be titled, 'Journey to Myself,' and it will include my life journey and experiences," Simmons said.

The launch date is not concrete yet, but Simmons urges individuals to be on the lookout for the book.

Willa Wyatt, the chair of the Friends of the Mars Hill Anderson Rosenwald School, shared more insight into the rehabilitation progress, and points out that the group's work is not done.

"Reaching out to the next generation of children and grandchildren of those who went to the Rosenwald school on Long Ridge and Stephens-Lee High School in Asheville to get their input on the school is extremely important," Wyatt said.

Wyatt said that the committee is looking forward to the PAGE (Partnership for Appalachian Girls' Education) program, hosted through Duke University, holding one week of their four-week summer session at the Mars Hill Anderson Rosenwald School.

Wyatt is also looking forward to the book about the history of the Mars Hill Anderson Rosenwald school being published in September 1, 2022, as well as a new program called Rhythm and Roots that will begin in February of 2022.

This spring, a major Rosenwald school exhibit has opened at the National Center for Civil and Human Rights in Atlanta, Georgia for individuals to come and learn the history of the schools.

Reprinted with permission of the News-Record & Sentinel.

Our Story, This Place

Mars Hill Rosenwald School Reclaimed

By Fay Mitchell for the North Carolina Department of Natural and Cultural Resources, December 9, 2019

Mars Hill Anderson Rosenwald School 2019

The almost forgotten Anderson Elementary School in Mars Hill is being reborn. It evolved from a school for Black children built in 1928 to enable African Americans still weighed down by the impact of slavery to seek a better life.

The Black community remained in western North Carolina as slavery ended for the small population of enslaved there. A split in pro-Confederate and pro-Union sentiment led many Blacks to move from Yancey to the Union-leaning Madison County at the Civil War's end.

For generations, as segregation limited options and opportunity for Blacks, the school, originally Long Ridge School, was a stepping-stone to life beyond the farm or the kitchen. Then integration happened and the school closed in 1965 to become a relic of a bygone time.

Such schools were the vision of Booker T. Washington, a Black educator and founder of Tuskegee Institute, who shared that vision of lifting Blacks out of poverty through education with Julius Rosenwald, president of Sears and Roebuck, who also had the vision and resources to help make it a reality. He created the Rosenwald Fund in 1917.

The fund provided capitol for 5,000 schools across the South, including 800 in North Carolina, more than any other state. Washington believed that self-help and education would lead to social mobility and better lives for Blacks, and Rosenwald concurred. To receive $750 grants, the community and school district had to raise matching funds for school construction. Many communities eagerly pitched in to make the dream of education come true for their children.

In 1930, Madison Elementary was known as the Long Ridge Rosenwald School and also welcomed Black students from Marshall. It had one open room that was divided into two spaces. One side was for grades one through four, the other for grades five through eight. The lone teacher moved between the younger and older students. The school served the region.

"Our bus went to Hot Springs, and I lived in Marshall," recalls Sarah Hart. "It wouldn't hold over 15 students. There were not that many of us."

In 1959 the school became Anderson Elementary, named to honor a local enslaved craftsman. Alumni of the school remember it fondly, as a place they got a good education, even if the books were all hand-me-downs of whatever was available. The teacher had lots of discretion, and when they had books of Shakespeare they read and performed Shakespeare—the entire school. She also taught about leaves and vines and the natural environment of the region. They started each day with prayer and devotion and felt a kinship as a family.

"That's where it all started," Hart continued. "I thought the school was so special. I am so glad it was saved."

The physical reminder of this history might have been lost. A farmer asked the Board of Education to demolish the dilapidated building in 2003. That request was denied, discussions began, and in 2011 the Friends of the Mars Hill Anderson Rosenwald School group was formed. There was a ribbon-cutting and celebration of rehabilitation progress in August 2019. The Madison County School Board is formulating plans to bring life again to this once vibrant structure.

The school was a stepping-stone to life beyond the farm or the kitchen.

Reprinted courtesy of the NC Department of Natural and Cultural Resources

The Story of This School Matters

It shows the dedication that Black residents of the Long Ridge community had for their children's education when they labored and raised money to help build the school.

It shows the care, commitment, and love that the Black teachers had for the students and community they served. It shows how the experiences of Black people in Appalachia have often been erased or overlooked, and how we must work to recover and highlight them. And it shows the absolute necessity for interracial understanding and cooperation if we are to achieve a more honest, just, and equal society moving forward.

The Mars Hill Anderson Rosenwald School has undergone major transformations in its lifespan, from 1928 until today. Many people—including MHARS alumni, current community members, historians, educators, students, and other friends of the school—have worked tirelessly to renovate the building, uncover its history, and share the meaningful stories that made the school significant to those who studied and worked there.

Students stand for a class photo outside the Mars Hill Anderson Rosenwald School.

Sarah Roland graduated from the school in 1953.

Mary H. Wilson taught at the school from 1939 until 1953.

Quilting Exhibit Honors the History of the Mars Hill Anderson Rosenwald School

A quilting and storytelling project, led by artist Jenny Pickens, became a lens for helping girls honor the stories of the school's alumni and former teachers.

Quilt square created by PAGE Program Director Maia Surdam.

Quilt square created by Anna Ingle.

Quilt square created by PAGE Project Facilitator Jenny Pickens.

Quilt square created by Wrenn Treadway.

Artist and educator Jenny Pickens believes that art can be a powerful force of healing, connection, and creative expression. She taught PAGE (Partnership for Appalachian Girls' Education) students how to sew by hand and how to use quilting to tell stories and preserve history. PAGE Program Director Maia Surdam worked with Jenny Pickens to help the girls create the quilt squares.

The new humanities PageLab, connecting history and the arts, took place inside the historic Mars Hill Anderson Rosenwald School two-room schoolhouse. Students learned about the teachers, community members, and alumni who taught at, supported, and attended the school. The students were able to hear stories about Mary Wilson, Frances Owens, Ruby Fortune, and Charity Ray.

To see the whole collection of quilt squares, and to listen to the stories behind each piece of art, go to pageprograms.com. You will hear PAGE students, interns, and teachers talk about their quilt squares and what inspired them.

The quilt squares shown here help preserve the legacy of the Mars Hill Anderson Rosenwald School.

Endnotes for Local and National Recognition

The Mars Hill Anderson Rosenwald school building has been rehabilitated by Black and White friends and neighbors.

Why Does This Place Matter? pg. 122

1. *American Library Quarterly*, Harry C. Boyte, "The Black Freedom Tradition and Libraries as Civic Commons," 2022; MHARS Friends Group Meeting (Member Ray Rapp Contribution) May 31, 2022.
2. Hasia R. Diner, *Julius Rosenwald: Repairing the World*, 2017.
3. *The North Carolina Historical Review*, Thomas W. Hanchett, "The Rosenwald Schools and Black Education in North Carolina, LXV, #4, October 1988; Barry Malone, "Divine Discontent: Nathan Carter Newbold, White Liberals, Black Education, and the making of Jim Crow South," University of South Carolina Doctoral Dissertation, 2013.
4. National Register of Historic Places, website, 2021.
5. Madison County Board of Education Minutes, July 1959, April 1963, May 1964; MHU Joseph Anderson Memorial Kiosk: "From Slave to Founder," Joe Anderson Drive, MHU Campus.
6. BOE Minutes, 1896 (1920-29) and 1907.
7. Moore Collection, MHU Archives, "MC Financial Record Book."
8. BOE Minutes, 1905-07.
9. Moore Collection, "MC Financial Record Book."
10. BOE Minutes, May 1953.
11. McLeod, *From These Stones*, 1968, Opposite p. 251.
12. BOE Minutes 1960-64.
13. MHARS Minutes 2014-22.
14. BOE Minutes, 1959, 1963, 1964.
15. BOE Minutes, 1905-64; Fisk University Rosenwald Records, 1928.
16. Emily Wilson, *Hope and Dignity, Older Black Women of the South*, pp. 168-175, 1983.
17. BOE Minutes, 1953-64; Ray Family History, "Family Reunion," 2000.
18. MHARS Minutes, 2009-18.
19. Ibid., 2008-18.
20. National Register of Historic Places, website, 2018.
21. MHARS Minutes, 2014-22, Fatimah´ Shabazz, Facilitator.

A display case of artifacts from the history of the building is part of the museum room at the school.

The school got a fresh coat of paint in 2017.

The school in 2019.

Appendix

The Historic Mars Hill Anderson Rosenwald School

Federal Census Data on the Joseph Anderson Family

Madison County, North Carolina

1860 Slave Owner Schedule

> Joe Anderson is listed in J.W. Anderson's 1860 Slave Schedule. The two males, ages 26 and 23, would be Lewis and Joe. The two children, ages 1, would be Andy and Cordelia, although they are listed as females.

Anderson, J. W.

57	M	B
60	F	B
26	M	B
23	M	B
18	F	B
17	F	B

14	M	M
9	F	M
1	F	B
1	F	B

Ray, T. W.

60	F	B
15	F	M
12	F	M

[Joe's Rays were from this family, J.W. Anderson's brother-in-law]

1870 Madison County Federal Census, Raysville

House #				
212	Ramsey, Willey	SC	(B)	35
	Eliza	SC	(B)	37
	Anderson, Cordelia		(B)	12 [Twin?]
238	Anderson, Isaac		(B)	65 [Father]
	Joseph		(B)	25
	Andy		(B)	12 [Twin?]
	Nelus		(B)	09
239	Anderson, Lewis		(B)	37
	Marinda		(B)	30
	Matilda		(B)	12
	Madison		(B)	09
	Albert		(B)	05
	Sopha		(B)	01

1880 Madison County Federal Census, #3 Bull Creek
[Near E. Carter/T. S. Deaver]

Joe's Brother

House #			(Age before June 1, 1880)
287	Anderson, Lewis	(B)	50
	Marinda	(B) wife	40
	Matilda	(B) daughter	20
	Mattison	(B) son	17
	Albert	(B) son	15
	Sophia	(B) daughter	11
	Lucinda	(B) daughter	09
	Samuel	(B) son	07
	John	(B) son	05
	Clara	(B) daughter	01

Joe's Second Family

House #				S	F	M
360	Anderson, Joseph	(B)	50	NC	MD	VA
	Mary	(Mu) wife	52	GA	ng	ng
	Delila	(Mu) daughter	21			
	Cornelius	(Mu) son	16			
	Henry	(Mu) son	13			
	Mary A.	(Mu) daughter	12			
	Dora L.	(Mu) daughter	07			
	Carr	(Mu) granddaughter	01			
	Ray, Susan	(B) mother-in-law	85			

Joe Anderson's family are listed in the 1880 Census, showing Joe's second family. Joe was born in NC; his father, Isaac Anderson, was born in MD; Joe's mother was born in VA.

The Historic Mars Hill Anderson Rosenwald School

African American History Time Line: The Long Ridge Colored Community

Students stand for a class photo outside the Mars Hill Anderson Rosenwald School.

1901

"Colored" schools at Mars Hill, Grapevine, and Ivy were operating at this time.[1] Two of the teachers in the early Mars Hill "Colored" School days were members of the Joseph Anderson family: Effie Anderson (Coone) was a teacher in 1901,[2] while nephew Sam W. Anderson was a teacher in 1905-06 and then from 1911-12.[3] He was the son of Lewis Anderson (Joseph's brother).[4] Joseph Anderson served on the Mars Hill Colored School Committee in 1896.[5] His son, Neal Anderson served on the committee in 1906-07.[6]

1905

The new Mars Hill Colored School building was built on Long Ridge and was referred to as the "Long Ridge School"[7] by alumni.

1907

Joseph Anderson died around this time and was buried in the Huff family graveyard. His grave was moved to Mars Hill College campus in 1932.[8]

1917

Mount Olive Baptist Church was begun in the school building, organized with 100 members, most of whom travelled over five miles to attend service, bringing memberships from Piney Grove Church on Walker Branch at Paint Fork of Little Ivy to the new church. The old Mount Olive Baptist Church building was erected in 1917.[9]

1928

The Madison County School Board purchased an additional acre of land on Long Ridge to meet the requirements for receiving support from the Rosenwald Fund.[10]

John Ferguson paid $200[11] for the community's match to receive the Rosenwald funds of $750.[12]

1929

The Long Ridge Rosenwald School, offering grades 1-8, was opened, located on the older, Long Ridge "Colored" School site.[13]

1930s

Mars Hill's Civilian Conservation Corp's "Camp Joe" on South Main Street to Long Ridge was named for Joseph Anderson.[14]

1936

Madison County School Board deeded land beside the school to trustees of the Mount Olive Cemetery: John Ferguson, Oliver Barnett, Jim Hampton, Rev. J. H. Smith, Pastor.[15] Annual "decoration of the graves" still takes place at Homecoming, the first weekend in September.

1940s

Viola King Barnette's letter to the NC Superintendent of Schools secured high school access for all rural students in North Carolina.[16] Her son, Herbert, and others from the Madison County, were bused to Stephens-Lee High School in Asheville.[17]

Rosenwald monies were secured in 1928 for what became the Mars Hill Anderson Rosenwald School.

The Historic Mars Hill Anderson Rosenwald School

Students at the Long Ridge School.

1959

The Long Ridge Rosenwald School was renamed Anderson Elementary School, in honor of Joseph Anderson.[18]

1961

Oralene Graves (Simmons), an alumna of the Rosenwald School, was the first African American student admitted to Mars Hill College in 1961. She is a great-great-granddaughter of Joseph Anderson.[19]

2009

The Planning Committee for saving the Rosenwald School building was formed.[20] (The Mars Hill Anderson Rosenwald School is the only Rosenwald school still standing in western NC.)[21]

2010

Architect Scott Donald of Padgett & Freeman Architects was commissioned by the Planning Committee to draw up plans for the rehabilitation of the historic Rosenwald school building.[22]

2012

A new roof was provided for the Rosenwald school building with help from Madison County School Board, the Conservation Trust of North Carolina partnership, and Mr. Lawrence Ponder.[23]

2011

2013

A Strategic Plan evolved and was adopted by the Mars Hill Anderson Rosenwald School Planning Committee. The committee also began the process of forming a 501(c)3 nonprofit corporation to help with fundraising.[24]

2014

MHU's Rural Life Museum opened its exhibition: "Our Story, This Place—The Mars Hill Anderson Rosenwald School Story," which ran from September 7, 2014 to February 28, 2015).[25]

2018

The Mars Hill Anderson Rosenwald School listed on the National Register of Historic Places.[26]

2018

A $50,000 rehabilitation grant was awarded by the African American Cultural Heritage Action Fund.[27]

2019

Mars Hill Anderson Rosenwald School Strategic Plan updated; Notated History Updated and Published; Grand Public Dedication, August 30-September 1, 2019.[28]

2013

2016

Water to the Long Ridge School

Girls pose for a class photo on the grass near the school.

From the Madison County Board of Education Minutes[1]

Feb. 6, 1939: A delegation from Long Ridge Colored school… requested the Board to install a water system… and pay water rent to the Town of Mars Hill for the use of said school.

Mar. 6, 1939: The Board ordered that the Superintendent purchase approximately 2,000 feet of ¾-inch galvanized pipe for Long Ridge School.

Jun. 5, 1939: A delegation from Long Ridge Colored school requested the Board take immediate steps… lay a pipe line from the Mars Hill water line to the school house.

Sep. 6, 1943: A letter was read from Mr. R.L. Lee (Mayor of Mars Hill) concerning the extension of pipe line to Mars Hill Colored school. The Board of Education approved the giving of $150.00 to the Town of Mars Hill to extend the pipe line. This amount was to be returned to the Board of Education in water rent from the Mars Hill Colored school. Among bills approved: Town of Mars Hill, water line, $150.

Oct. 4, 1943: Board of Education approved the agreement. The Mars Hill Colored school will receive water free of expense until the $150.00 will have been used at the rate of $4.00 per school month.

Jan. 3, 1949: The Board was informed that contract with Town of Mars Hill to supply water to Mars Hill Colored school until $150.00 had been consumed was fulfilled and a letter from Mr. Lee, Mayor of Mars Hill, stated charge would continue to be $4.00 per month water rent. The Board considered the amount too much and directed Supt. contact Mr. Lee requesting reduction in water rental for Mars Hill Negro School.

Feb. 7, 1949: The Town of Mars Hill has agreed to charge the minimum of $2.50 per month for water rent for Mars Hill Colored School.

Mar. 7, 1949: Among bills approved: Town of Mars Hill, water (Colored school), $9.63.

Time Line for Education in Madison County Area

1793-1832	Old Buncombe County "Old Field Schools,"[1] Madison County area (log school buildings erected in worn-out farm fields)
1833	Yancey County established, included Madison County area
1840-1850	Buncombe/Yancey County "Common Schools," including Madison (NC statewide free public schools for Whites)[2]
1851	Madison County established
1856-1859	French Broad Institute/Mars Hill College[3]
1860s	Madison County "Subscription Schools" (parents subscribed to pay teacher with corn, wheat, or ham)
1870s	Peabody Schools in Madison County (Grantville, Forks of Ivy; Pleasant Hill, Mars Hill; Laurel Branch)[4]
1874	Free Public Schools in Madison County (20 White schools and one Black school)[5]
1887-1909	Northern Presbyterian Schools in Madison County[6]
1900s-1920s	Secondary Education in Madison County: Marshall High School; Hot Springs High School; Walnut High School; Laurel High School; Spring Creek High School; Ebbs Chapel High School; Beech Glen High School; Mars Hill High School
1928-1965	Mars Hill Anderson Rosenwald School to Madison Integration
1974-1975	Madison County High School[7]

Log school buildings were erected in worn-out farm fields in the early 1800s.

The Historic Mars Hill Anderson Rosenwald School

Mixed Early Ethnic Heritage History of Mars Hill College[1]

Oral tradition claims that Joe and other enslaved men may have helped make the bricks for the first Mars Hill College building, which was completed in the spring of 1856. The building was torn down in 1910.

1856

During MHC's first ten years, 1856-1865, its ethnic heritage history is a mixed ethnic story. Of the twenty-two known Founding Families, sixteen had no slaves; four families had domestic slaves, one, two and four; while two Founding Families had more: Henry Ray was one of the largest enslavers in Yancey County, while the J.W. Anderson family of Madison County enslaved ten, whose chattel included the young Joe Anderson family. Joe was the individual for whom the Rosenwald School was named.[2]

1859

Anderson's slave Joe was taken in 1859 as collateral on the college debt to the contractors who erected the first building.[3] Finally, a Madison County court order cut the debt from $3,000 to $1,100 because of poor workmanship. The Buncombe County sheriff, with the contractors, levied against J.W. Anderson, taking Joe to jail in Asheville, until the debt was paid.[4]

- Eleven of the Trustees met in the college building to deal with the crisis. John Ammons, son of Trustee Stephen Ammons, was present for the meeting, as recorded in his history book in 1907, "with their faces in their hands."[5] They agreed to share the debt equally among them, which would save Joe from a slave-block-sale, and return him to his young family in Mars Hill, "that being accomplished in a few Days." Two Trustees rode horseback, a three-day trip, to Spartanburg, SC and Statesville, NC to borrow each his $100 dollars.[6]
- For these Trustees, it was not just a financial crises for MHC and enslaver Anderson, but a moral judgement decision for themselves.

1850s

"The Rev. Thomas Jefferson Rollins left SC to Mars Hill in protest against slavery, his having witnessed a young Negro girl's being cruelly whipped. Seeing her lacerated back, he swore he would no longer live in a place where such conditions existed!"[7]

- Another reason the Rev. Rollins family moved to Mars Hill was that they and their SC Baptist church members had enjoyed fellowship with most of the mountain Baptist families who would later found MHC in 1856. They belonged to the Big Ivy Baptist Association of Churches, 1827-1849.[8] Those MHC Founding Churches were the Middle Fork church; the Liberty Church of Big Ivy; the Gabriel's Creek Church; and the Fork of Ivy Church.[9]

- In 1827, the French Broad Baptist Association of Churches was ripped asunder when the Rev. Garrett Deweese, pastor of Middle Fork Baptist Church, was expelled from the Association because he preached the doctrine of Free Salvation, not just for the Elect, and the Autonomy of the Individual Believer, as well as the Elect. Deweese led in organizing the Big Ivy Baptist Association of Churches. His Middle Fork Church followed him, as did six other churches. During the next two decades, the Association grew to twenty-five churches.[10]
- The division between the two Associations was settled in 1849, when the Big Ivy Baptist Association's Article of Faith, "Autonomy of the Individual Believer" was accepted. Peace advocate Daniel Carter, prayers answered, went Home in peace.[11]
- While living in Mars Hill, the Rev. Rollins' son, Pinkney Rollins, married Hester Deaver, daughter of Trustee Thomas Shepherd Deaver, who also abhorred slavery; thus, joining two strong Union families.[12] Soon after, Pinkney Rollins became president of Mars Hill College in 1861.[13]

1861-1865

When the Civil War broke out, the Greater Mars Hill Area was divided between the two causes, forcing the college to close. During the War, Confederate soldiers were headquartered in the college buildings, until Union soldiers came in and burned two of the three college buildings.[14]

1865-1870

After the War, during Reconstruction, outlaws from both sides, North and South, continued the War's devastation, casting neighbor against neighbor, and brother against brother, leading to what became the Ku Klux War!"[15] A nearby mountain was named the Ku Klux Mountain, located by Walker Branch on Paint Fork of Little Ivy in Madison County, as a result of the KKK's lingering influence in the area.[16]

- Trustee Thomas Shepherd Deaver organized the Union League in the college building to protect the freed Blacks and the returning Union soldiers.[17] The KKK saw Deaver as a traitor and attacked him and the Union League, threating his person, his family, his home, and his mills at the Forks of Ivy.[18] Finally, his mills were burned in 1866.[19]

During the War, Confederate soldiers were headquartered in the college buildings, until Union soldiers came in and burned two of the three college buildings.

The Historic Mars Hill Anderson Rosenwald School

African and Native American Ethnic Heritage at Mars Hill University

Mars Hill College in 1909

1905 – President Moore of Mars Hill College, while serving as Superintendent of Madison County Schools with the Board of Education, built a new Mars Hill Colored Elementary school building in what became the Long Ridge Community in Mars Hill,[1] consolidating Mars Hill, Grapevine, and Ivy Colored schools.[2] The Long Ridge Community and Mount Olive Baptist Church evolved around this new school building.[3] This building would be replaced in 1928 with the new Rosenwald School building.[4]

1920s – Mars Hill College accepted students of Color, Native American and Foreign.[5]

1922 – Rev. Dr. Walter N. Johnson, a Stewardship leader in the Southern Baptist Convention and beginning in 1922, professor in Mars Hill's Department of Religion. He helped organize the interracial Minister's Conference held at Mars Hill, 1930-1950, and his pamphlet, "The Next Step," was printed at Mars Hill and mailed to Christian leaders through the South.[6] College historian John Angus McLeod called him "a prophetic Christian philosopher of his day."[7] The Social Gospel ministry which he espoused had a profound impact on the Civil Rights Movement in the South, and with Christian leaders nationally.[8]

1922-44 – Dr. Walter Johnson's "The Next Step" was published at Mars Hill College for Christian ministers throughout the South.[9]

1928-31 – Rev. Dr. Martin England was professor of Religion and Math at Mars Hill College.[10] Having come under the influence of Dr. Walter Johnson, he became active in the Social Gospel Movement and, in 1942 helped Clarence Jordan to found Koinonia Farm, an interracial community in Sumter County, Georgia.[11] Out of this community came "The Cotton Patch Gospel" by Jordon and "Habitat for Humanity" by Milton Fuller. Further, Dr. England was called "The Johnny Appleseed of the Peace Movement," because of his work nationally for peace, especially in the Civil Rights Movement with Dr. Martin Luther King Jr.[12]

1928-29 – MHC President R.L. Moore serves as Chairman of the Board of Education in Madison County for its new Mars Hill Anderson Rosenwald School, which credits his leadership with two new African American school houses in the Long Ridge Community.[13]

1930s – From Dr. Johnson's influence during the 1930s:

- Churches in Hickory Mill villages were integrated.[14]
- Black and White ministers from across the South came to summer meetings at Mars Hill College;[15] many of whom became Christian leaders in the southern integration movement during the 1960s.

- MHC contributed influences to the "Social Gospel" movement in the South.
- Koinonia, a 1942 interracial community in Georgia was founded by Clarence Jordan and Martin England.[16]

1932 – During the Moore Administration and with the leadership of Professor McLeod, Joseph Anderson's grave was moved to the Oak Grove near the south entrance to Mars Hill College campus, with an appropriate granite Memorial Marker, "In Memory of Joe."[17]

1933 – Mars Hill College integrated its summer conferences in this year, with southern church leaders coming to the college, both White and Black, men and women.[18]

1938 – Mars Hill College employed African American residents of the Long Ridge Community: Dallas Anderson and sister Doskey Anderson McDowell, grandchildren of Joe Anderson, began work in the new college cafeteria kitchen.[19]

1940s – Dr. Blackwell accepted Native Americans from eastern North Carolina, the Croatan/Pembroke/Lumbee, into Mars Hill College.[20]

1940s – College personnel, Caroline and Martha Biggers, with Vann, encouraged African American laundress Viola King Barnette (MHU Coach Kevin Barnette's grandmother) to write to the North Carolina Superintendent of Schools seeking Colored students' access to high school, resulting in all North Carolina rural children's access to high school.[21]

1953 – Dr. Jim Jones, a Lumbee Indian, after graduating from MHC went on to medical school and later became head of the Department of Family Practice at East Carolina University Medical School.[22]

1961 – Oralene Graves (Simmons) was accepted to Mars Hill College,[23] the first African American accepted by the school, making it the first Baptist School in North Carolina to fully integrate.[24] She is the great-great-granddaughter of Joseph Anderson, the slave who went to jail in 1859 for a college debt owed to the contractors on the first academic building.[25] Ms. Simmons is retired Executive Director of the YMI Cultural Center in Asheville, NC.[26] She organized the Martin Luther King, Jr. Prayer Breakfast in Asheville, NC, the largest in the southeast.[27]

1960s – Nine to twelve other African American students attended Mars Hill College during the 1960s.[28]

1968 – Significant academic programs that benefited minorities were begun by Academic Dean Dr. Richard Hoffman. The Upward Program began at the college in the Summer of 1968 with 55 high school students on campus for eight weeks. Ten of those students were African American students from Asheville City Schools and one from Mars Hill. Two of these nine students became very successful. Dr. Joe Crawford became a medical doctor in New York City and Audrey Byrd Mosley became a highly successful attorney in Washington, DC. The purpose of the Federal Upward Bound Program was to encourage disadvantaged high school students to attend college. Dr. John Hough, Chair of the Education Department, wrote the federal grant proposal and became the first director of the program at Mars Hill.[29]

Oralene Graves (Simmons) was the first African American accepted to Mars Hill College.

> Sarah Roland Weston Hart, a native of the Long Ridge African American Community in Mars Hill, graduated with a degree in Elementary Education from MHC, being the first to graduate from the Long Ridge Community at MHC.

1971 (Aug.) – Patricia Brown Griffin graduated from Mars Hill College, becoming the first African American to graduate from the senior college. Ms. Griffin studied in the COP Program with Dr. John Hough. She transferred to Mars Hill from Stillman College in Tuscaloosa, Alabama. She worked in the Asheville City School System after receiving her BA from Mars Hill College and MA from Western Carolina University in Elementary Education. She served as the Principal of the Randolph Learning Center. She also taught in adult classes at Mars Hill College in 1996 and 1997. Patricia Brown Griffin is now retired, living in Asheville.[30]

1970-1975 – The Career Opportunity Program (COP) was an innovative initiative that provided the education training needed by teacher's assistants to become fully certified teachers. The COP Program was written by Sylvia Airhart, from Mars Hill, Supervisor for the Asheville City Schools, and Dr. John Hough, Associate Dean for Academic Affairs at Mars Hill College, who also served as Director of COP from 1973-1975. The program served some 200 teachers' assistants in the Asheville City, Buncombe County and Madison County School Systems. It graduated 125 of these students as fully certified teachers who taught in the three school systems. Over 60 of these were African Americans who taught in Asheville City and Buncombe County School Systems, becoming graduates of the Mars Hill COP Program. In 1975 the COP Program became the Continuing Education Program, directed by Mr. Ray Rapp.[31]

1972 (May) – Three African American students graduated from Mars Hill College in 1972:

- Rodney Lynn Johnson, Asheville High School athlete, received a BS in Physical Education, and worked until his retirement at George Washington University.[32]
- Sammy Lewis Lucas, from Lamar, South Carolina, received a BS in music education and voice.[33]
- Roger David McGowan, from Laurens, South Carolina, received a BS in biology.[34]

1975 – Sarah Roland Weston Hart, a native of the Long Ridge African American Community in Mars Hill, graduated from MHC with a degree in Elementary Education, being the first African American to graduate from Madison County and her Long Ridge Community. She taught school in the Asheville City School System from 1975-1984. Moving to Virginia, she taught school in Alexandra, VA, and in Prince William County where she received her Masters Degree in Organizational Leadership Management from George Mason University. After retirement, Sara returned home to NC in 2007. Her granddaughter, Stephanie Weston, continued her family education tradition by graduating from MHU in 2007. Sarah Roland Weston Hart is an alumna of the Mars Hill Anderson Rosenwald School and Stevens-Lee High School in Asheville. Today, she is serving as a member of the MHARS' Friends Group and their History Committee.[35]

1981 – Charlene Delores Ray was the first Joseph Anderson descendant to graduate from Mars Hill Senior College; she was a great-granddaughter of Doskey McDowell, granddaughter of Joseph Anderson.[36] Ms. Ray was the first Appalachian Scholar at Mars Hill College. Her Scholar's Research was entitled "History of Blacks in Madison County, 1860-1981," now in the school archives.[37] She graduated with Honors and while at Mars Hill was named to Who's Who in American Colleges and Universities.[38] After she received her Master's Degree at Eastern Tennessee State University, Mrs. Charlene Ray Dunn was employed at the Environmental Protection Agency in Washington, DC.[39]

1986 – MHC integrated its Bailey Mountain Clog Team when Dr. Donald Anderson placed Reggie Dixon, an African American student, on the team, making Bailey Mountain the first Appalachian clog dance team to integrate in the South.[40]

1995 – Namurah Simmons, daughter of Oralene Graves Simmons, graduated from Mars Hill College.[41]

1999 – Joseph Anderson and the Jane Ray Family was designated a Mars Hill College Founding Family.[42]

2006 – Joe Anderson Memorial Site listed on the National Register of Historic Places.[43]

2009 (May) – Shamia Terry, granddaughter of Oralene Graves Simmons, graduated from Mars Hill College.[44]

2010 (Oct.) – East Dormitory Drive on the University campus was re-named Joe Anderson Drive to further honor Joseph Anderson.[45] MHU Founders Week celebrated the Joseph Anderson Family, meeting in the Long Ridge Community at Mount Olive Church and Mars Hill Anderson Rosenwald School.[46]

2011 – President Dan Lunsford and Principal Chief Michel Hicks of the Eastern Band of Cherokees signed Heritage Agreement in support of Scholarships and Historic Resources for Cherokee students attending MHU.[47]

2013 – Mars Hill College graduate Rodney Lynn Johnson, an African American, was named Mars Hill University Alumnus of the Year.[48]

2014 – MHU students received the National Picture Award, taken by Dr. Mullinax, for their Community Service at the Rosenwald School during the American Martin Luther King Day of Service.[49]

2015 – Weeping Cherry Tree planted during Founders Week by MHU NAACP students at the Joe Anderson Memorial to honor Oralene Graves Simmons.[50]

2017 – Joseph Anderson Kiosk "From Slave to Founder" was erected at the Anderson Memorial.[51]

2018 – 217 African American and 17 Native American students were enrolled in the MHU student body of 1,132.[52]

2019 – Public celebration of Mars Hill Anderson Rosenwald School Ten Year Rehabilitation Milestone at Mars Hill University, the Long Ridge Community, and at the Rosenwald school.[53]

2020 – Unveiling Our Treasures, "From Margins to Center: Reflections on the History of African Americans at Mars Hill University, 1856-1980," by Dr. David Gilbert and Malik Frost. Their presentation was given at the Liston B. Ramsey Center at MHU.[54]

2022 – Oralene Anderson Graves Simmons is awarded an Honorary Doctorate by Mars Hill University.[55]

Namurah Simmons Blakely

Peabody Education Fund in North Carolina

George Peabody is widely regarded as the father of modern philanthropy.

Founded of necessity due to damage caused largely by the American Civil War, the Peabody Education Fund was established by George Peabody in 1867 for the purpose of promoting "intellectual, moral, and industrial education in the most destitute portion of the Southern States."

"We pay for well-regulated public free schools, continued about ten months of the year, and having a regular attendance of not less than 100 pupils, averaging daily 85 per cent."[1]

The following North Carolina schools were accepted for funds in the 1874-75 school year:

Fayetteville	$450	Balsam Seminary	300
Flemming's Chapel	300	Rich Hill	300
Shoal Creek	300	Ivy*	300
Roan Mountain	300	Smyrna	300
Pisgah	300	Smithfield	300
Flat Creek*	300	McElrath Chapel	300
Webster	300	Waynesville	300
Cowee	300	Holly Springs	300
Grantville* (Forks of Ivy)	300	Charlotte "Colored"	300
Pleasant Hill* (Mars Hill)	300		
Laurel Branch*	300		

* Of the twenty schools in North Carolina that qualified for Peabody Funds, five (20%) were in the greater Mars Hill area: only one "Colored" Peabody school in the whole state.

Schools for African Americans in Asheville, North Carolina

Allen High School opened on October 31, 1887.

During segregation in the 1940s, African American children were barred from attending White schools, and in Madison County there was no Black high school; the Long Ridge School in Mars Hill went only from first through seventh grade. Their only option was to attend school in Asheville.

Allen High School[1]

The Allen High School was built for African Americans by Mr. and Mrs. Pease, who retired to Asheville, NC, from New York City. According to Julia Titus, principal of the school from 1938 to 1967, the lack of educational facilities for Negroes "became a burden on the hearts of the Peases." Paying all costs and expenses, the Peases built the school, which opened October 31, 1887, with the Reverend N.S. Albright and Alsie B. Dole as teachers. The first day, three people were enrolled. By the end of the month enrollment climbed to 103, and by the close of its first year, more than 200 students were enrolled. Children attended during the day, older people at night.

As the school grew, so did the need for additional buildings. The women of the Woman's Home Missionary Society conceived of a home where girls could learn. Mrs. Marriage Allen, wife of an English Quaker philanthropist, visited the school while touring the South. She was so impressed by the work being done that she offered to give $1,000 if the Society would build the home at once. It was done, and on February 9, 1897, Allen Home was dedicated.

In 1941, Allen Home became a project of the Woman's Division of Christian Service, and in June 1945, the name was officially changed to Allen High School. In 1924, Allen became a four-year high school with accreditation from the state of North Carolina and in 1940 received accreditation by the Southern Association of Colleges and Secondary Schools.

Stephens-Lee High School[1]

Stephens-Lee High School, the "Castle on the Hill," was built in Asheville in 1921.

In 1921 ground was broken in Asheville, NC for Stephens-Lee High School for African American students. The gym, built in 1940, is shown in a photo from approximately 1947. The "Castle on the Hill," home of the "Bears," was completed in 1922 and welcomed its first students in the Spring of 1923. Edward Stephens became the first principal of the segregated School.

Stephens-Lee was named after George Henry Stephens, the first Black principal in Asheville (Catholic Hill High School), and Mrs. Hester Lee, the wife of Walter Smith Lee, the second principle of Catholic Hill (destroyed by fire in 1917). Stephens-Lee attracted and educated many of the area's brightest students including nationally known and Ivy-League-educated scholars. The class of 1924 was the first graduating class, and the class of 1965 was the last.

With no public notice, the school building was demolished in April, 1975, but after vocal and determined protests against the city, the gym was saved, and today serves as the Stephens-Lee Recreation Center.

School Books Recommended by State Board of Education for the Year 1886[1]

Title	Price
Holmes' First Reader	.14
Holmes' Second Reader	.24
Holmes' Third Reader	.36
Holmes' Fourth Reader	.48
Holmes' Fifth Reader	.80
Holmes' New History of the U.S.	1.00
Maury's Elementary Geography	.60
Sanford's Primary Analytical Arithmetic	.20
Sanford's Intermediate Analytical Arithmetic	.36
Sanford's Common School Analytical Arithmetic	.64
Sanford's Higher Analytical Arithmetic	1.00
Worchester's Primary Dictionary	.48
Worchester's Common School Dictionary	.80
Worchester's Comprehensive Dictionary	1.40
Worchester's Academic Dictionary	1.50
Worchester's Octavo Dictionary	3.46
Reed & Kellogg's Graded Lessons in English	.40
Reed & Kellogg's Higher Lessons in English	.70
Goodrich's Child's History of U.S.	.60
Stephens' History of U.S.	1.08
Swinton's Language History Primer	.28
Harringtons' Spelling Book	.20
Moore's History of N.C.	.85
Steele's Abridged Psychology	.50
Beers' System of Penmanship, per doz.	1.20
Harrey's Revised Elementary Grammar	.50

The Mars Hill Anderson Rosenwald School was a Rosenwald Funded School, while others were only Rosenwald designed school buildings.

School Names Noted in Board of Education Minutes

The Mars Hill Anderson Rosenwald School name evolved over the years in the Madison County Board of Education Minutes. "Our Story, This Place," used in the Museum Exhibit and Notated History, was first used as the theme in the Strategic Plan in 2013.

Madison County, North Carolina 1905-1966

Board of Education Minutes related to the "Mars Hill Colored School," also known as the "Long Ridge" and "Anderson School"—A Rosenwald Fund School.

Note different names used for the school

Jan 2 & 3, 1905	Mars Hill Colored
July 9, 1928	Work on "Negro" School Building
1928–29	Budget Year, Fisk University Rosenwald Fund, Card File Historic Name: Mars Hill School
Feb. 6–June 5, 1939	Long Ridge Colored School
April 1, 1940	Mars Hill Colored School
Jan 3, 1949	Mars Hill Negro School
July 6, 1959	Superintendent, Fred Anderson, to request Colored School Committee to select an appropriate name for the Colored school that would add more prestige and dignity to the school
April 1, 1963	Committee: "Mars Hill Colored School was to be named at a later date."
May 4, 1964	First entry in the Board of Education Minutes naming the Mars Hill Colored School as the Mars Hill Anderson (Colored) School.
April 5, 1965	Anderson Colored School, Mars Hill Anderson School
April 27, 1965	Anderson School

School Committee Persons

In 1896 there were five "Colored" School Districts in Madison County.

1896 "Colored" School Committeemen Madison County, North Carolina[1]

Marshall	Hot Springs	Little Pine Creek	Bull Creek (Mars Hill)	Middle Fork
Wm. Williams	Joe Logan	Henry Paine	Joe Anderson	Joe Logan
M. Roberts	Ned Ray	Mark Baker	Alfred Bailey	Ned Ray
Lon Henry	Ben Hampton	John Paine	J.B. Bailey	Ben Hampton

Mars Hill "Colored" School Committeemen 1896–1913[2]

1896 Bull Creek: Joe Anderson; Alfred Bailey; J.B. Bailey (Mars Hill P.O.)

1896 Middle Fork: Joe Logan; Ned Ray; Ben Hampton (Briggsville P.O.)

Five "Colored" School Districts in Madison County: Mars Hill, Middle Fork, Ivy, Marshall, and Hot Springs

1905 Ivy: A.D. Coon; Howe Ray; Jerry Wilson

1905 Mars Hill: J.H. Ferguson; Alfred Barnett; Neil Anderson

1906 Ivy: A.D. Coon; Howe Ray; Jerry Wilson

1906 Mars Hill: Neal Anderson; Alfred Barnett

1910 Mars Hill: James Bowdridge

1911 Ivy: W.B. Ray; Harvey Ray; Dolph Coon

1913 Ivy: W.B. Ray; Harvey Ray; Dolph Coon

Arseamous "Seam" Roland

Manuel Briscoe

Augusta "Gustie" Briscoe Ray

Known Mars Hill "Colored" School Committee Persons 1937–1964[1]

1937: Gilbert Briscoe; Alfred Barnett; Oscar Young

1939: Oscar Young; Gilbert Briscoe; Alfred Barnett

1940: Oliver Barnett; Oscar Young; Gilbert Briscoe

1941: Oscar Young; A. M. Roland; A. E. Ray

1953: Gustie Ray; Avery Ray; Dowell Anderson

1957: Avery Ray; Seam Roland; Gustie Ray

1958: Gustie Ray; Avery Ray; Seam Roland

1960: Manuel Briscoe; Augusta Ray; Seam Roland

1961: Manuel Briscoe; Augusta Ray; Seam Roland

1962: Seam Roland; Augusta Ray; Manuel Briscoe

1964: Manuel Briscoe, Chair.; Seam Roland; Augusta Ray

Mars Hill Integration "Colored" School Committee[2]

This School Committee assisted the Madison County Board of Education for a peaceful integration of the schools in 1965.

Manuel Briscoe, 1964 Chairman, 1960-65, was Town of Mars Hill employee, brother to Augusta Ray, married to "Little Frances" McDowell, great-granddaughter of Joe Anderson.

Arseamous "Seam" Roland, 1957-65, first Long Ridge Community landowner in 1939, father of Sarah Hart.

Augusta "Gustie" Briscoe Ray, 1953-65, sister to Manuel, mother of Charity Ray and Dorothy Coone.

NB: 1953 Committee: "Gustie" Ray, only female appointed, 1896-1965; Avery Ray, ancestor of Rev. Ray; Dowell Anderson, Joe's grandson, married to "Big Frances" Roland, Joe's granddaughter-in-law; "Committee recommended the hiring of a new teacher."

School Teachers

Mars Hill "Colored" School Teachers 1901–1913[1]

1901	Effie Anderson (Fall)
1902	Eliza L. Randolph
1903-04	Elise Rand (Eliza Randolph?)
1905-06	Sam W. Anderson
1906-07	Sam W. Anderson
1907-08	Sallie Green
1908-09	J.B. Baile
1909	Josephine Barnard
1910	Alice Baird
1911-12	Sam W. Anderson
1912-13	Sam W. Anderson

Effie (Coone) Anderson, granddaughter of Joseph Anderson, taught at the school.
Photo courtesy of John Campbell

> By 1929 there were just three "Colored" Schools in Madison County.

African American School Teachers of Madison County, North Carolina: 1924-1965[1]

School Year	Teachers (Salary) Mars Hill	Teachers (Salary) Hot Springs	Teachers (Salary) Marshall
1924-25	[blank]	Elizabeth Coleman	M.K. Page[2]
1926-27	Frances E. Gilliam ($75)	Mrs. J.E. Coleman ($45)	Willie E. Kyle ($25)[3]
1927-28	Sallie Mae Mackey ($45)	Mrs. J.E. Coleman ($45)	W.K. Page ($75)[4]
1928-29	Gertrude Roseboro (65) [present building]	Mrs. J.E. Coleman ($45)	Flora Lucky ($45)[5]
1929-30	Charity Hazzard ($45)	Mrs. J.E. Coleman ($45)	Flora Lucky ($45)[6]
1930-31	Charity Hazzard ($45)	Mrs. J.E. Coleman ($45)	Flora Lucky ($45)[7]
1932-33[8]			
1935-36	Elizabeth Conley; Edna Bell	Mrs. J.E. Coleman[9]	
1936-37[10]			
1938-39	Mrs. Wilson [1 teacher]	Mrs. J.E. Coleman [1 teacher][11]	
1939-40	Mrs. Mary H. Wilson [1 t]	Mrs. J.E. Coleman[12]	
1940-41	Mary H. Wilson [1 t]	Mrs. J.E. Coleman [1 t][13]	
1941-42	Mrs. Mary H. Wilson [1 t]	Grace Owens [1 t][14]	
1942-43	Mrs. Mary H. Wilson [2 t]	Frances M. Owens [1 t][15]	
1943-44	Mary H. Wilson; Ida Long Sigmon [2 t]	Frances M. Owens [1 t][16]	
1944-45	Mrs. Mary H. Wilson [2 t]	Frances M. Owens [1 t]17	
1945-46	Mary H. Wilson; Addie J. Best [2 t]	Frances M. Owens [1 t][18]	
1946-47	Mrs. Mary H. Wilson [2 t]	Frances M. Owens [1 t][19]	
1947-48	Mrs. Mary H. Wilson [2 t][20]	[No Hot Springs Negro school from 1947-48 forward]	

School Year	Teachers (Salary) Mars Hill
1948-49	Mary H. Wilson [2 t][21]
1949-50	Mary H. Wilson; Grace Owens [2 t][22]
1950-51	Mary H. Wilson; M. Grace Owens [2 t][23]
1951-52	Mary H. Wilson; M. Grace Owens [2 t][24]
1952-53	M.H. Wilson, Principal; M.G. Owens, Teacher [2 t][25]
1953-54	Mary H. Wilson; M. Grace Owens [2 t][26]
1954-55	Mrs. Lillie D. Love [1 t][27]
1955-56	Bernice Smith [1 t][28]
1956-57	Mrs. Smith [1 t][29]
1957-58	Bernice S. Smith, Principal [1 t][30]
1958-59	Bernice E.S. Smith, Principal [1 t][31]
1959-60	Bernice E.S. Smith, Principal [1 t][32]
1960-61	Mrs. Dora B. Bass [1 t][33]
1961-62	Dora B. Bass, Principal & Teacher [1 t][34]
1962-63	Dora B. Bass, Principal & Teacher[35]
1963-64	Mrs. Maggie P. Brown[36]
1964-65	Maggie P. Brown [1 t] Anderson School[37]

Mary H. Wilson was hired to teach at the school in 1939.

The Historic Mars Hill Anderson Rosenwald School

Effie Anderson (Coone), a teacher at the Mars Hill School, was the granddaughter of Joe Anderson and the grandmother of Oralene Simmons.

Madison County School Expense Records

Book 1901–1904, Box 103, Folder 1[1]

YEAR	SCHOOLS	Excerpts and Notes by Richard Dillingham
1904	**Marshall Colored**	These books are expense ledgers saved by Dr. Moore, Superintendent of Madison Schools, 1901–1912.
	M.E. Moore (Mar. 15–Apr. 30)	
	William Sullivan	Mars Hill College Archives, Local History, Box 103, Folders 1–3.
	Little Pine Colored	(Transferred to Marshall)
1901	**Marshall Colored**	
	Albert Logan	
	M.E. Moore	
1901	**Mars Hill Colored**	
	Effie Anderson (Sept.–Oct 4)	Granddaughter of Joe Anderson (Effie Coone), grandmother of Oralene Simmons
	E.L. Randolph (Sept.–Dec.)	
	Eliza Randolph	
1901	**Ivy Colored**	May have been located on Walker Branch between Paint Fork and Middle Fork Communities, where the Black Piney Grove Church building was located.
	Joseph Logan	
1902	Joseph Logan	
1904	Joseph Logan (Feb.)	
	Joseph Logan (Aug.)	
1902	**Hot Springs Colored**	
1901	**Grassy Knob (White School)**	Located below the Long Ridge Community on Old NC 213, knoll above Flint Morgan Drive in the Forks of Ivy Community.
1901	**Grapevine Colored**	
	J.B. Bailey (Dec.)	Stepfather of Viola King Barnette
1903	J.B. Bailey (Jan.)	

Book 1903–1908, MHC Local History Archives, Box 103, Folder 2[2]

YEAR	SCHOOLS	Excerpts and Notes by Richard Dillingham
1903	**Hot Springs Colored**, p. 109	
1904		
1905		
1906		
1907		
	Ivy Colored, p. 65	
1903	Joseph Logan	
1904	Joseph Logan	
1905	Joseph Logan	
1906	Joseph Logan	
1907	Elise Randolp	
1908	Sallie Green	
1908	J.H. Coone	
1909	J.H. Coone	
1903	**Marshall Colored**, p. 27	
1909	**Mars Hill Colored**, p.151	
1903	Elise Rand	
	Elise Rand	
	Elise Rand	
1904	$125 Bld. & Lot	I believe this was allocated for what became the Long Ridge School Building and lot. Land deed from Scudder Willis and new school building would be the first construction in what would be the Long Ridge Community.
1905	Sam W. Anderson	This is believed to be the son of Lewis, brother to Joe.
	Sam W. Anderson	
1906	R.S. Gibbs expense for Repair	
	Sam Anderson	
1907	Sallie Green	
	Sallie Green	
	Sallie Green	
	Neal Anderson was paid .64 for School Census. He was son of Joe Anderson.	

> **In 1905 it was reported that a school house had been erected for the "Colored" people of Mars Hill at a cost of $125 including an acre of ground.**
>
> ~ *from the Madison County Board of Education Minutes*

Sam W. Anderson, a teacher at the school, was the nephew of Joe Anderson.

YEAR	SCHOOLS	Excerpts and Notes by Richard Dillingham
1908	J.R. Rogers was paid $10.50 for road	I suspect this was for Old School Road, before Mt. Olive Drive was located. J.R Rogers sold the land for Mt. Olive Church to be built.
	J.B. Bailey	
	J.B. Bailey	
	J.B. Bailey	
	J.B. Bailey	
1909	J.B. Bailey	
1905	Unused appropriations, $125, set aside for buildings in districts, p. 163	
	Mars Hill Colored (Jan. 1905)	

Ledger for 1909–1912, Box 103, Folder 3[3]

1911	**Hot Springs Colored,** p. 106	
1911	J.B. Bailey teacher	
	J.B. Bailey teacher	
1909	**Marshall Colored,** p. 26	
	J.B. Bailey teacher	
1909	**Mars Hill Colored,** p. 146	
	Josephine Barnard, teacher	
1910	A.B. Barnett was paid .64 for School Census	
1910	Alice Baird, teacher	
	Alice Baird, teacher	
1911	S.W. Anderson, teacher	
1912	S.W. Anderson, teacher	
	S.W. Anderson, teacher	
	S.W. Anderson, teacher	
	S.W. Anderson, teacher	

Notes on Integration

Madison County Board of Education Meetings

September 6, 1963:

Action: Consider Geraldine Griffin's request that her child be assigned to Asheville School Unit

Decision: Rejected

April 6, 1964:

Action: Consider Geraldine Griffin's written request to place her child in the Mars Hill White School

Present: Geraldine Griffin, Mother

Board of Education

Mr. Day, Asheville Attorney, NAACP

Mr. Roland, Colored Jeweler of Asheville

Anderson Rosenwald School Committee

Manuel Briscoe, Chairman

Seam Roland, Augusta Briscoe Ray

Decision: Meet Again June 1, 1964

Jesse Ray

> The decision to allow Geraldine Griffin's child to attend the Mars Hill White School was approved on June 1, 1964.

Madison County Board of Education Meetings[1]

June 1, 1964:

Action: Consider Geraldine Griffin's written request.

Present: Jesse Ray of Asheville

Board of Education

Mr. Eldridge Leak, County Attorney

Long Ridge School Committee

Manuel Briscoe, Chairman

Seam Roland, Augusta Ray

(Media) Mr. Shields, WMMH Radio

Mr. Story, News-Record

Mr. Harlecheck, Asheville Citizen

Decision: Meet again at 9:30PM

June 1, 1964, 9:30PM Meeting:

Action: Consider other written requests by parents.

Present: Jesse Ray of Asheville

Board of Education

Mr. Roland of Asheville

Long Ridge School Committee

Manuel Briscoe, Seam Roland, Augusta Ray

Mars Hill Parents: Gudger Barnett, Mrs. Irene McDowell, Mr. Ernest Ervin; Marshall was Mrs. Presnell and three children

Decision: Approved

Jean Dobbins, 1st Grade, to M.H. School (Father, Gudger Barnett)

Phillip M. Ervin, 7th Grade to M.H. School (Father, Ernest Ervin)

Betty & Anne McDowell, 7th Grade to M.H. School (Mother, Irene McDowell)

Vickie Louise Wilson, 5th Grade to M.H. School (Mother, Geraldine Griffin)

Endnotes for Appendix

African American History Time Line: The Long Ridge Colored Community, pp. 140-143

1. Madison County School Expense Records, MHC Local History Archives, Box 103, Folder 1.
2. Ibid. Box 103, Folder 1 (Sept.-Oct.).
3. Ibid. Box 103, Folder 2, p. 151; Folder 3, p.146.
4. Federal Census, Madison County, NC, Bull Creek, 1880.
5. MCBOE Minutes, 1907; Office of County Commissioners, 1896.
6. MCOBE Minutes, 1905-1907.
7. Edwin Cheek Interviews: Shirley Sewell; Augusta Ray; Manuel Briscoe, 1983.
8. Stephen Chandler, "The Story of Joe Anderson, the Slave at Mars Hill College," MHC History Paper, 1990, MHC Archives.
9. Madison County Heritage Book, Vol. 1, p. 32.
10. Biennial Report of Supt. of Public Instruction of NC, Part III, 1929-1930, p. 314.
11. Oral Interview with Dorothy Ray Coone, 2012.
12. Fisk University, "Rosenwald Fund, Card Database," Dan Slagle.
13. Ibid.; Cheek Interviews, 1983.
14. Harley Jolly, That Magnificent Army of Youth and Peace…, p. 46 (Raleigh, NC: Edwards Brothers Printers), 2007.
15. Madison County Deeds, 1936.
16. Emily Wilson, Hope and Dignity: Older Black Women of the South, pp.172-173.
17. Cheek Interview, Sewell, 1983.
18. MCBOE Minutes, 1959.
19. John Angus McLeod, From These Stones, p. 251 (Mars Hill, NC: Mars Hill Press), 1968; Reprint 2000.
20. Rosenwald Planning Committee Minutes, Dec. 2009.
21. Ibid., Fisk.
22. Ibid., RPC Minutes, 2010.
23. Ibid., RPC Minutes, 2012.
24. MHARS Strategic Plan, 2013; 2019.
25. Rural Heritage Museum Exhibit: Our Story, This Place, 2014-2015.
26. National Register of Historic Places, 2018.
27. African American Cultural Heritage Action Fund, 2018.
28. Grand Public Dedication, August 30-September 1, 2019.

The Anderson Rosenwald School closed in 1965.

The Historic Mars Hill Anderson Rosenwald School

The French Broad Baptist Institute became Mars Hill College in 1859.

Water to the Long Ridge School, p. 144

1. *Madison County Board of Education Minutes, Feb. 6, 1939-Mar. 7, 1949; extracted by Pauline Cheek and Dan Slagle.*

Time Line for Education in Madison County Area, p. 145

1. *Miller, Education in Buncombe County.*
2. *Hunter, Education in Yancey County.*
3. *McLeod, From These Stones.*
4. *NC Annual Report, pp. 54-57.*
5. *Ibid. NC Annual, p. 101.*
6. *Underwood, This Is Madison County, opposite p. 43.*
7. *Willa Wyatt, M.C. School Teacher, Interview, 2020.*

Mixed Early Ethnic Heritage History of Mars Hill College, p. 146-147

1. *Richard Dillingham, Copyright, June 19, 2021.*
2. *Sams, McLeod, From These Stones, p. 19; Dillingham, MHC Beginnings…, pp. 3-9; 1860 Federal Census Slave Schedules, Madison/Yancey Counties, NC; Madison County Board of Education Minutes, 1958.*
3. *John Angus McLeod, From These Stones, "John Robert Sams' History," p. 19, 1968; Edward Jennings Carter, "A History of Mars Hill College," M.A Thesis, UNC Chapel Hill, MHU Archives, p. 8, 1940.*
4. *Madison County Court Records, 1859; Steve D. Chandler, "The Story of Joe Anderson Revisited," a Senior History Thesis, MHC, pp. 8-11, MHU Archives; McLeod, p. 21.*
5. *John Ammons, "Outlines of History of French Broad Baptist Association and Mars Hill College," p. 89. 1907.*
6. *McLeod, p. 19.*
7. *Ibid., p. 68.*
8. *Ammons, "Ministers;" Big Ivy Baptist Association Minutes and Liberty Baptist Church Minutes, 1830s/1840s, Baptist Collections, MHU Archives.*
9. *McLeod, p. 68; Richard Dillingham, "MHC Beginnings: History Briefs, Connecting the Dots to Founders and Churches, pp. 10-16, 2007.*
10. *Ammons, p. 13; Garrett Dewees Dialogue, 1827, Baptist Collections, MHU Archives.*
11. *Ammons, p. 16.*
12. *McLeod, p. 61.*
13. *Ibid., p. 49.*
14. *Ibid., p.68.*
15. *Ibid., pp. 88-89.*
16. *Map of Madison County, NC by T.V.A., 1934, Research by Dr. David Gilbert.*
17. *Dillingham, History of Forks of Ivy, 2013.*
18. *Dr. William Logan's Family Journal by Julia Ann Deaver Logan, daughter of T.S. Deaver and wife of A.L. Logan.*
19. *Dan Slagle, Research: "Thomas Shepherd Deaver vs. James A. Keith," Buncombe County Court Records, 1868-1876.*

African and Native American Ethnic Heritage at Mars Hill University, p. 148-151

1. MCBE Minutes, 1906.
2. Ibid.
3. MC Land Records, J.R. Rogers, 1925, Slagle.
4. Op. Cit., Minutes, 1928-29.
5. MHC Family Portrait, The Laurel, 1921.
6. John A. McLeod, From These Stones, pp. 270-271, 1967; Ken Sanford, The Mystique of Mars Hill, p. 47, 2007.
7. Ibid. p. 270.
8. Beverly England Williams, By Faith and By Love, 2015.
9. Ibid.
10. Sanford, p, 48, England "The Next Step,"1941.
11. Ibid., p. 48.
12. Williams, Addendum, Dr. Albert Blackwell Funeral Comments of England.
13. MCBE Minutes, 1928.
14. McLeod, p. 270.
15. Ibid., p. 271.
16. Williams, 2015.
17. McLeod, pp. 23-24.
18. Ibid., p. 271.
19. Ibid., Opposite p. 251.
20. Ibid., pp. 268-69.
21. Emily Wilson, Hope and Dignity: Older Black Women of the South, pp. 172-73, 1983.
22. Ken Sanford, "The Mystique of Mars Hill, Interview with Dr. Chapman, p. 80, 2006.
23. McLeod, Opposite p. 251.
24. NC Historical Review, "Integration of Baptist Colleges in NC."
25. Stephen Chandler, "The Story of Joe Anderson Revisited," Student Research, 1988, MHU Archives.
26. Leigh Anne Rhodes, "Simmons shares lessons of equality with MMS students," News-Record, pp. 1A, 8A, Feb. 12, 2018.
27. Sam DeGrave, "MLK, Jr. breakfast founder delivers keynote address," Asheville Citizen-Times, p. 3A, Jan. 14, 2018.
28. Walter Smith, MHC Public Relations, MHU retiree.
29. Dr. John Hough, Upward Bound Program Director, Interview 2021.

In 2010, East Dormitory Drive on the campus of Mars Hill University was renamed Joe Anderson Drive in honor of Joseph Anderson.

The rehabilitated Mars Hill Anderson Rosenwald School includes technology for presentations to school groups.

African and Native American Ethnic Heritage at Mars Hill University, p. 148-151

30. Chapman Interview, 2009, Hough Interview, 2021.
31. Dr. Hough, Ray Rapp Interviews, 2021.
32. Chapman, Registrar Records, 2009.
33. Ibid.
34. Ibid.
35. Sarah Hart Interview, 2021.
36. MHARS "Our Story, This Place," p. 40.
37. Ibid.
38. Ibid.
39. Ibid.
40. MHC Registrar Records, Anderson, Music 469, BMC.
41. Ibid., 1995.
42. Joseph Anderson Kiosk "From Slave to Founder," 2017.
43. National Register of Historic Places, 2006.
44. MHC Registrar Records, 2009.
45. MHC Founders Week, October 12, 2010.
46. Ibid., 2010.
47. MHU News, Online, 2011.
48. MHU Homecoming, 2013.
49. MHARS, "Our Story, This Place," p. 51.
50. MHU Founders Week, October, 2015, Anderson Kiosk.
51. MHU Founders Week, 2017.
52. MHU News, Online, 2018.
53. MHARS Celebration, "Our Story, This Place," pp. 50-53.
54. Dr. David Gilbert, "Unveiling Our Treasures," MHU Liston B. Ramsey Center, 2020.
55. MHU Graduation, May 2022.

Peabody Education Fund in North Carolina, p. 152

1. *NC Annual Report of the Superintendent of Public Instruction, Nov. 1, 1874-75, p. 57.*

Schools for African Americans in Asheville, North Carolina, pg 153

1. *The Urban News,* "History of African Americans in Buncombe County," September 2015.

Stephens-Lee High School, p. 154

1. *The Urban News,* "History of African Americans in Buncombe County," September 2015.

School Books Recommended by State Board of Education for the Year 1886, p. 155

1. *Biennial Report of the Superintendent of Public Instruction of NC, 1885-1886, p. 5.*

School Committee Persons, p. 157-158

1896 "Colored" School Committeemen Madison County, North Carolina, p. 157

1. *Madison County School Board Minutes, 1907: Office of County Commissioners, 1896.*

Mars Hill "Colored" School Committeemen 1896–1913, p. 157

2. *1896 "Colored" School Committeemen Madison County, North Carolina.*

Known Mars Hill "Colored" School Committee Persons 1937–1964, p. 158

1. *Madison County BOE Minutes, 1905–1965.*

Mars Hill Integration Colored School Committee, p. 158

2. *Madison County BOE Minutes, 1953-1965. Extracted by Pauline Cheek and Dan Slagle; 1953 BOE Minutes; Dillingham Notes.*

African American teachers were paid more to teach at Rosenwald schools than at other schools for Black students.

School Teachers, p. 159-161

Mars Hill "Colored" School Teachers 1901–1913, p. 159

1. *School Expense Ledger Book, Folder 3.*

African American School Teachers of Madison County, North Carolina: 1924-1965, p. 160-161

Sources: News Record; Board of Education; NC Directory of School Officials for each school year from Internet Archives site.

1. *Compiled by Dan Slagle in October 2015 and September 2021.*
2. *News Record.*
3. *News Record, School assigned to is assumed – not stated in newspaper.*
4. *Ibid.*
5. *Ibid.*
6. *News Record, Transporting students from Marshall to Mars Hill, @ Supt. C.M. Blankenship, BOE Chair: R.L. Moore.*
7. *News Record, Another teacher: Ruth Littlejohn, * Three schools in Oct. 1930.*
8. *Board of Education, Discontinue 8th grade at Mars Hill Colored School.*
9. *Board of Education.*
10. *Board of Education, Oscar Young contracted to haul students from Marshall to Mars Hill.*
11. *Board of Education; NC Directory of School Officials.*
12. *Board of Education, Oscar Young and Xavier were paid transportation supplement.*
13. *Board of Education; NC Directory of School Officials, one teacher each school.*
14. *Board of Education; NC Directory of School Officials, Supt. G.B. Rhodes.*
15. *Board of Education, Dec. 1942, rent was paid for Hot Springs Colored School; NC Directory of School Officials, M.H. two teacher, H.S. one teacher.*
16. *Board of Education, Aug. 1943, Ida Long Sigmon resigned, 1944, rent paid for Hot Springs C.S.; NC Directory of School Officials [2 t], [1 t].*
17. *NC Directory of School Officials.*
18. *Board of Education; NC Directory of School Officials.*
19. *NC Directory of School Officials.*
20. *Ibid.*

African American School Teachers of Madison County, North Carolina: 1924-1965, p. 160-161

21. *Board of Education; NC Directory of School Officials.*
22. *Board of Education; NC Directory of School Officials, Supt. Mrs. Edna G. Rhodes, Chair, J. Clyde Brown.*
23. *Board of Education; Sarah Roland's report card; NC Directory of School Officials.*
24. *Board of Education; NC Directory of School Officials.*
25. *Sarah Ann Roland's Certificate of Promotion to High School; NC Directory of School Officials.*
26. *Board of Education; NC Directory of School Officials.*
27. *News Record, May 5, 1955, newspaper refers to "the Colored School" in the county; Board of Education; NC Directory of School Officials.*
28. *Board of Education, Building was a one classroom unit; NC Directory of School Officials.*
29. *News Record, Dec. 27, 1956, "our Colored school" mentioned in newspaper; NC Directory of School Officials.*
30. *News Record, Board of Education; NC Directory of School Officials.*
31. *Board of Education; NC Directory of School Officials.*
32. *Board of Education, Janitor, Avery Ray, Bus drivers Manuel Briscoe, Marshall; Eugene Briscoe, Asheville; NC Directory of School Officials.*
33. *Board of Education; NC Directory of School Officials.*
34. *NC Directory of School Officials, grades taught 1-6.*
35. *News Record, Board of Education; NC Directory of School Officials, grades taught 1-6.*
36. *Board of Education, Janitor, Seam Roland, June 1, 1964, decision to integrate five students to Mars Hill White School; NC Directory of School Officials, grades taught 1-6.*
37. *Board of Education, April 27, 1965, Decision: "Anderson School will be closed at the end of this school year;" NC Directory of School Officials, grades taught 1-6.*

Madison County School Expense Records pg. 162-164

1. *Madison County School Expense Records, Mars Hill College Archives, Local History, Box 103, 1901–1904, Folder 1.*
2. *Ibid. Box 103, 1903–1908, Folder 2.*
3. *Ibid. Ledger 1909–1912, Folder 3.*

Madison County Board of Education Meetings, p. 166

1. *Madison County Board of Education Minutes, Sept. 6, 1963–June, 1964. Extracted by Pauline Cheek and Dan Slagle*

More Rosenwald buildings were built in North Carolina than any other state, a total of 813 by the program's conclusion.

~ The Historic ~
Mars Hill Anderson Rosenwald School

Standing in front of the old Mt. Olive Church. Photo courtesy of Augusta Ray

**To contribute stories or funds to the project,
please visit www.marshillandersonrosenwaldschool.org**